501 THINGS TO DO IF YOU DARE

Dangerous Hobbies for Fearless People

BEN MALISOW

foreword by Troy Hartman

METRO BOOKS
NEW YORK

This book contains material adapted and abridged from
1001 Things to Do If You Dare, copyright © 2007 by Ben Malisow.

This 2009 edition published by Metro Books,
by arrangement with F+W Media, Inc.

Cover design and illustrations by 3&Co.

Metro Books
122 Fifth Avenue
New York, NY 10011

ISBN: 978-1-4351-2163-8

Printed and bound in the United States of America.

10 9 8 7 6 5 4 3 2 1

Interior illustrations: background grunge texture ©istockphoto.com / maigi, cigarette burn ©istockphoto.com / michael1959, coffee mug ring ©istockphoto.com / ranplett, road sign © istockphoto.com / JulienGrondin, instant photo frame © istockphoto.com / zcw26, instant photo frame with tape © istockphoto.com / samgrandy.

CONTENTS

INTRODUCTION

Many of the things in this book are dangerous. No, really—participating in some of these activities can lead to serious harm, permanent injury and disfigurement, or even death. Some of them are incredibly stupid, some are probably criminal in most locales, and some are just criminally stupid. The author has done some of these things; others he wouldn't do if you promised him cotton candy and sexual favors for a hundred years. The number of skulls ☠ following the activities listed in this book denotes the author's estimation of difficulty/insanity/stupidity of that particular item—**1** for things that your grandmother could probably accomplish, **5** for things that are just ludicrously dangerous and inane.

The author, editors, publishers, and everyone affiliated with them do not recommend you try any of these, and, if you do, warn you that you do so at your own risk, and, furthermore, that we will have very little sympathy for you when you get hurt. We told you so.

There is something immensely satisfying, however, about participating in an activity that is inherently dangerous (and "dangerous" is used here not just to describe the possibility of physical harm, but psychological, emotional, and financial damage). There's the adrenaline rush, the view of one's own mortality, the welcome relief at the successful conclusion of the act. There is often a strange thrill of accomplishment, a self-congratulatory sensation, even when it's completely unwarranted (such as is earned by skydiving, which really isn't anything you, yourself, have done well, but is more a simple act of gravity and the expertise of the 'chute manufacturer). We like to scare ourselves. We like to push our own boundaries. We like to take risks, sometimes even foolhardy ones.

Most people aren't aware that vertigo isn't really a fear of heights. Vertigo, instead, is a fear of edges. There is something tucked away at the base of our snake brain, some little sensor that has been honed over eons to protect the animal that carries it; this instinctual device screams at us when we're about to do something that is quite obviously a threat to life and limb. This alarm system lets you walk up to the edge. It will even let you peek over. But if you start to consider leaping, this ancient security protocol will scream at you, telling you that the action you're contemplating is quite ill-advised. It can fiddle with your psyche as well as your biology, causing a myriad of reactions, from uncontrollable panting to muscle spasms to realistic visions of tragic outcomes.

This thing is meant to protect you. You can have great fun by poking it a few times and telling it to get bent.

Pick an edge; an actual edge, like a cliff, or a waterfall, or pick a metaphorical edge, like the limits of your patience or bravery. Go up to that edge, peer out over. Let your safety mechanism tell you how silly you're acting.

Then jump.

Part 1: Public Things

Performing a daring Thing where someone can see you is perhaps more frightening than doing it somewhere free from view; there is the additional fear of embarrassment to hinder you. Of course, depending on the audience, you may also get a group of people who egg you on.

SPEED, HEIGHT, DEPTH, AND MOTION THINGS There's something almost universally thrilling about moving your body at high velocity . . . probably because it was never designed to do so.

1 Ride a roller coaster.

☠

For an added thrill, do it without holding onto the restraints.

2 Drive the Autobahn.

☠ ☠ ☠ ☠

A wide, well-maintained road with no speed limit? Mama, sign me up! In some places there are speed limits (and concessions made for conditions throughout), but it's mainly a megafreeway with no restrictions on your lead-foot instinct.

THE AUTOBAHN WINDS THROUGH SWITZERLAND, AUSTRIA, AND GERMANY.

3 Bury the speedometer needle of a car.

☠ ☠ ☠ ☠

Take a vehicle somewhere desolate, where it would be impossible to harm another person (or somewhere it's allowed, like a racetrack). Rev it up, cut loose, and press the pedal all the way down. Keep it depressed until the speed indicator exceeds the highest number on the device. (As a challenge to the extra-stupid: Do this in a vehicle with a digital speedometer.)

4 Drive a motor vehicle on a frozen lake.

☠ ☠ ☠ – ☠ ☠ ☠ ☠ ☠ depending on conditions

Lakes often freeze without uniformity—meaning some spots are usually softer/thinner/more brittle than others. Take a life vest.

5 Put a car up on two wheels.

☠ ☠ ☠ ☠ ☠

Okay, maybe you're so cool you can pull this off . . . but can you get it back down, on all four wheels?

6 Drive a forklift.

☠☠☠

Those big prongs sticking out the front can really wallop someone or something, so be extra careful; even if you drive your car like an expert, it's tough to get a feel for where the front of the forklift actually is.

IF YOU'RE LUCKY, YOU CAN GET A FORKLIFT EQUIPPED WITH REAR WHEELS THAT TURN, INSTEAD OF THE FRONT SET, MAKING STEERING THAT MUCH MORE TRICKY.

7 Bungee jump.

☠☠☠

This was a practice originated by some South Pacific islanders, who were evidently incredibly bored with living in a glorious, unspoiled tropical paradise. Or they were under the influence of serious narcotics. My bet's on the latter. This is just plain stupid. I've had mixed results in my experiences with rubber bands . . . why would I trust one to withstand the weight of my body at terminal velocity?

8 BASE jump.

Put on a parachute. Climb to the top of a Bridge, Antenna, Span, or mountain/hill/cliff (the E is "Earth"). Jump. Deploy parachute. Congratulations: You're officially nuts.

9 Do a HALO jump.

This is a High-Altitude, Low-Opening skydive. Go way, way up into the sky—say, 20,000 feet—jump out, freefall for a good, long while (and distance!), then pull the cord when you're way too close to the ground (usually under the 2,500-foot "floor" for normal parachuting). Be sure to bring oxygen, an altimeter, and warm clothing.

10 Sky-surf.

☠ ☠ ☠

Skydiving—while standing on a board. I am not sure why there is so much focus on boards, when it comes to the various "extreme" sports. A latent construction fetish? The mind boggles.

Ride a motorcycle.

☠ ☠ ☠

Without a helmet. In traffic. In the rain. More than one rider will admit, sheepishly, after many drinks and some familiarity with the listener, that they've accomplished wondrous, crazy, awesome stunts on a bike, only to dump it while trying to park the damned thing.

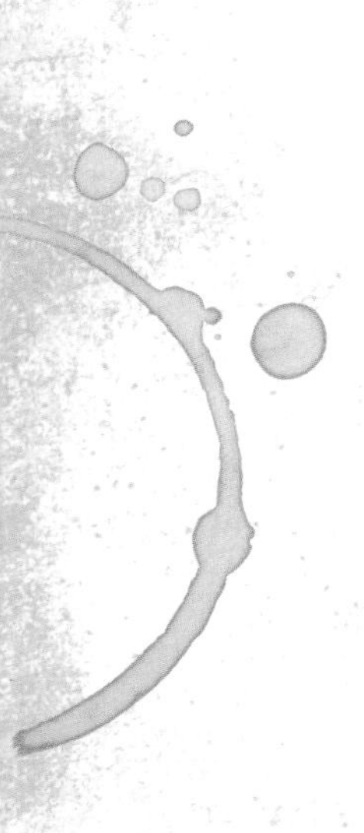

12 Wingwalk.

☠☠☠☠☠

Some people used to do this on a regular basis, back in the early days of flying. They go up in a plane (almost always with an open cockpit/cabin), then get out and crawl/pull themselves along the outside surfaces of the aircraft, in a display of bravery and stupidity. I can't fathom the reasons why.

13 Fly a hang glider.

☠☠

See, most people would think this would be more dangerous than flying a plane, because there's no engine. Actually, that's what makes it safer: there's no high-tech moving parts to worry about, no fuel to burst into flame and incinerate the pilot, much fewer things to go wrong.

IT'S A BETTER RIDE THAN FLYING A PLANE: TOTALLY SILENT, EXCEPT FOR THE WIND RUSHING PAST THE CANOPY. MAGIC. AWESOME.

14 Ride in a small jet with less than three seats.

☠☠☠

Pilots, especially jet pilots, especially Air Force jet pilots, are odd people, with a strange collective sense of humor. So they'll do things like tell you to look out the right side of the canopy, then yank the stick hard to snap your helmeted noggin into the other side of the canopy. They're weird creatures. Yes, they are.

15 Bail out of an aircraft with an ejection seat.

☠☠☠☠☠

Basically, you're sitting on a considerably high-powered explosive charge. When you fire that puppy, it's going to blast you into the air; if the aircraft is aloft, you're going to hit the airstream pretty much instantaneously, which is not like the mainly stationary air you feel around you most of the time.

AFTER ALL THAT, YOU'VE STILL GOT TO HOPE THE PARACHUTE OPENS, AND THAT YOU LAND INTACT.

16 Crash a vehicle.

☠☠☠☠☠

Writers lie—time does not slow down when an accident is imminent; if it did, you'd be able to respond in time to avoid the collision. Instead, time kind of telescopes. . . . There's a brief jumble during the instant before the crash itself, then the crash, then there is a portion of time immediately subsequent in which the prior fifteen seconds or so are clearly delineated in your mind's eye, and you can zoom in and out on any given detail. It's weird. But if you walk away, what a rush!

17 Drag race.

☠☠

There are racetracks that allow just anybody off the street to come in and try racing their own vehicles. Their insurance will probably cover anything that happens to them. Yours won't.

#16

Drive the wrong way down a one-way street.

☠ ☠ ☠

Sometimes—just sometimes, mind you—there are places you have to be, in cities expressly designed to keep you from getting to them. Sometimes circumstances conspire to make your destination unreachable. Sometimes you just have to decide to dismiss convention and legality, and just get to where you're going by going the wrong way.

ODDLY, MANY OF THE OPPOSING DRIVERS ARE FORGIVING. DON'T LET THIS GIVE YOU FALSE SECURITY; REMAIN WARY UNTIL YOU ACTUALLY GET WHERE YOU'RE GOING.

Drive in a foreign country.

☠ ☠

The rules are pretty much the same on roads everywhere in the world. It's not the rules you have to worry about—it's the accepted practices. There are nuances to driving, things all drivers in a certain place just happen to know, but aren't posted on any sign or in any rulebook. Don't look for help at the rental car desk, either. Try not to kill anyone. Or be killed, of course.

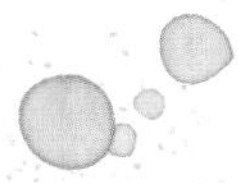

20 Cross a Las Vegas street outside of a crosswalk.

One of the few places on the planet where you will be cited, posthumously, for jaywalking, if a vehicle does indeed strike you dead. Sure, pedestrians still have the right of way, no matter what, no matter where, but law enforcement in this rather libertarian town frowns on those who cross against the light (or anywhere other than in prescribed locations). As long as the driver doesn't flee the scene, they're likely to get off with a stern warning and a slap on the wrist—while you, the pedestrian, are likely to be sundered.

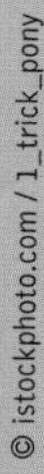
© istockphoto.com / 1_trick_pony

Enter a highway via the off-ramp (or exit via the on-ramp).

☠☠☠

There was an accident. Or a large event that is about to begin or has just ended. The roads pointed in a certain direction are jammed beyond capacity. You must get on (or off) the highway—it is essential. The only possible route is prohibited by law and common sense. Go slow, but get it done and get out of there.

Learn to drive a tractor-trailer rig.

☠☠☠

There's something about double-clutching involved, I think. That's the practice of using an unsynchronized manual transmission. There's also the necessity of an engine brake (called a "Jake brake") and/or air brakes, as truck braking systems don't use hydraulics. I know it's not just the same as driving a regular car. At least, I don't think so. Anyway, it seems pretty tricky. There are special schools for it and everything.

23 Ride a riptide.

☠ ☠ ☠

Large bodies of water do funny things. For instance, they sometimes create riptides, strong currents of water capable of dragging something fairly large and semibuoyant (you) from near the shore out to deeper waters. You can try to fight and probably drown, or you can go with it and enjoy the trip, then swim carefully, parallel to the shore, back to the beach. Your choice.

24 Go over a waterfall.

☠ – ☠ ☠ ☠ ☠ ☠, depending on conditions

The Thing of mythic proportions is the ride over Niagara Falls in a barrel. It is also a pretty sure-fire way to off yourself. So, unless you're looking for a flamboyant means of self-euthanizing, you might want to start with a tiny little waterfall of six feet or so, in a boat, while wearing a life jacket.

YOU CAN WORK UP TO THE LIFE-THREATENING WATERFALLS; THEY'LL STILL BE THERE WHEN YOU'RE READY TO DIE.

Ride a cigarette boat.

You know these things: the type of watercraft that drug smugglers like to use. You're not so much riding across the waves as skipping across them, like a stone flung sideways. And, like that stone, you can tip sideways and flip repeatedly.

Go underwater in a submarine.

, depending on circumstances

Sure, when you're diving, there's just as much chance something could go wrong . . . but you're probably deeper underwater when in the submarine. And you're trapped inside. There are just a few places where a tourist can find a submarine to ride: There's a provider called Atlantis Adventures (which spooks me, 'cause I remember where the term *Atlantis* comes from), Disneyland, and—formerly—the Edmonton Mall.

EDMONTON YANKED THEIRS IN 1998, SO HURRY AND GET TO ONE OF THE OTHERS, BEFORE THEY GET CANCELED, TOO.

27 Go off-roading.

☠ ☠

There's a reason we have roads. Roads are good: They are, for the most part, level, flat, and smooth, and engineered to support the weight of automobiles. Once you go off-roading, well, you're going off the road. In a vehicle. Which really isn't the purpose of the vehicle, nor the nonroad part of the planet. Hopefully, you've got roll bars. And plenty of drinking water.

28 Ride a snowmobile.

☠ ☠ – ☠ ☠ ☠ ☠ ☠, depending on circumstances

Only Americans would come up with the idea of plunking the internal combustion engine into a tracked vehicle to scoot across the snow. It was a Wisconsinite who came up with this notion (and the very best people, as we all know, come from Wisconsin). Carl Eliason got the first patent for his converted Model T Ford in 1927. The most powerful snowmobiles can now also skim across the water if the speed is high enough, but even this book doesn't recommend something as insane as that.

29 Walk on a ledge between two buildings, or two rooms of a building.

☠☠☠☠

Extremely similar to the foolishness of a tightrope, but here you have the added benefits of a structure wholly inappropriate for the purpose. For extra insanity, try it in the rain or wind or snow. I had a college roommate who rappelled off the top of the dorm building to wash the outside windows of his fourth-floor dorm room. Why? "Because they were dirty," he explained. Of course.

30 Get shot out of a cannon.

☠☠☠☠☠

Explosives aren't really featured in this activity, but they might as well be. Riding a shove from compressed air or an elastic slingshot, the human cannonball flies through the air to—hopefully—land in a net. There are easier ways to kill yourself.

31 Jump out a window.

☠–☠☠☠☠☠, depending on height

Notice I didn't say "jump through a window," because that's just suicidal, no matter how it's presented in the popular media.

ATHLETIC THINGS The human body is an amazing tool. On the one hand, it's an incredibly durable, time-tested vehicle for survival, capable of withstanding ridiculous amounts of punishment and privation. On the other hand, it's very delicate, and can be rendered inoperable through any number of relatively innocuous means. We like to explore the limits of the body's capacity for pain, exertion, and stress; we call this "athleticism." Push your own body through a series of activities that force it to the extreme parameters of endurance, neglect, and determination.

32 Ski down a double black diamond run in the Rocky Mountains.

☠ ☠ ☠ ☠

These ain't your dinky Appalachian Smokeys. Not some floofy European Alps. These are the no-kidding, gonna-kill-ya, 17,000-foot dagger-toothed monsters. They mean business. But with the altitude and the Colorado sun, you might be able to do it comfortably in jeans and a windbreaker. Cool.

33 Try kite-surfing.

☠☠☠

Like demented followers of a Ben Franklin cult, these people fly a kite while surfing. The kite drags them across the water and high up into the air, allowing them to do crazier things than if they were just surfing. Where's lightning when you need it?

34 Go bodysurfing in the ocean.

☠

The ocean doesn't play around. It's not your friend—it doesn't care about you. Your ancestors left it about 400 million years ago, and it's never forgotten that slight. Why should it? Did you ever write? Or call? No, you thankless chump. So the ocean ain't gonna be nice to you, either. You quickly become aware of that fact when it grabs you, drags you under, churns you up a bit, and spits you out onto shore. But man, is that fun! An inexpensive entertainment, as long as you live near an ocean.

35 Mountain-boarding.

Yep. Mountain-boarding. For when there's no snow, of course. Addicts needed a way to fulfill their boarding jones even in July, so some clever person stuck a few wheels on a giant skateboard, and now participants can scoot down a mountain of dirt, sans snow.

36 Swim against the current of a river.

The river moves; that's what rivers do. They move. They, themselves, move, and they move stuff, too. They move a whole bunch of stuff. Rocks, dirt, mountains. See that Grand Canyon thingy? That was the work of a river.

YOU THINK THE RIVER'S GOING TO HAVE MUCH PROBLEM MOVING YOU? WHAT DO YOU THINK YOU ARE? A SALMON? YOU'RE NOT A SALMON.

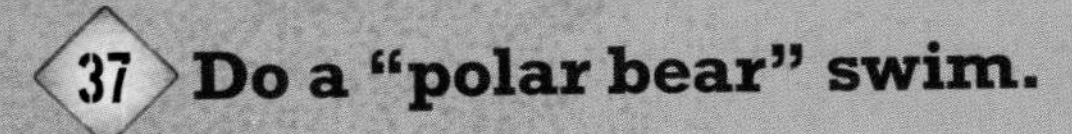

37 Do a "polar bear" swim.

☠

Pick a really cold place, during the cold season. Get up early in the morning, and go out to a body of water large enough to immerse yourself. Take off your clothes. Jump in. Get out, dry off, and go home.

LEAVE YOUR SHOES ON, OR YOUR FEET WILL STICK TO THE ROCKS ON THE WAY OUT.

38 Swim beneath an underwater obstacle of indeterminate length.

☠☠☠–☠☠☠☠☠, depending on distance and circumstances

Find out just how long you can hold your breath. Feel your lungs rebel against the tyranny of your idiocy. Let your sinuses attack your skull in various ways. Make sure you get to the other side of whatever it is you're swimming under.

39 Go snorkeling.

☠ – ☠ ☠ ☠, depending on conditions

The snorkel is an awesome invention, allowing a swimmer/diver to look down into the water and still breathe. It can also funnel saltwater directly into your throat and lungs. Know what you're doing.

40 Rappel out of a helicopter.

☠ ☠

Surprisingly, this is a lot easier than the rappelling involving a mountain. There's no edge, especially if you start the activity by sitting in the open doorway of the chopper, your legs dangling out into space. You're looking down at the ground where you started (before the helicopter lifted off), but, after a hundred feet or so, you don't really have any concept of height—your depth perception doesn't work like that. So jumping is easy. Make sure to bark the "Hut-hut-hut" sounds from *The Blues Brothers* as you do it. Just check to see that the rope reaches the ground before you leap; if it does, landing is easy.

41 Go barefoot in a wintry setting.

Ice and snow don't complement human flesh. In addition to the threats of frostbite and abrasion, your extremities (in which your feet are included) radiate a great deal of body heat, and you can easily end up with a good case of hypothermia, which is a pretty straightforward way to die.

42 Climb a building ("buildering").

–, depending on conditions

Every now and then, some a--hole in a crazy costume (usually Spiderman) tries to climb one of the world's tallest buildings. You, too, can be an a--hole. Just pick a building and start climbing. Buildings that have been climbed by various a--holes: the Sears Tower, the Sydney Opera House, the Eiffel Tower, the Empire State Building, and the National Bank of Abu Dhabi.

BUILDERING IS USUALLY ILLEGAL, AND WILL RESULT IN YOUR ARREST. IF YOU SURVIVE.

43 Run a footrace.

Who's the fastest human being present? Whoever runs fastest, of course. I, personally, run fastest when being chased, so the footrace thing hasn't really worked for me in the past.

44 Run a marathon.

Somebody, hundreds of years ago, picked an arbitrary distance, a distance which the human body was not designed to travel quickly or comfortably, and made it a fad.

© istockphoto.com / millsrymer

45 Juggle sharp objects.

☠☠☠☠

Because nothing is nearly as impressive as slicing open your flesh in front of strangers.

46 Jump a horse.

☠☠–☠☠☠☠, depending on conditions

No—there's no way you can jump over a horse. I mean you should ride the horse over a jump, of course. People have been doing this for a long time—and horses have been doing it even longer. So it's nothing new. But if it's new for you, it's pretty wild. Unless you fall off, mid-jump, of course.

47 Play pato.

How do I explain? . . . Okay. This is a combination of basketball and polo. Two teams of horseback riders try to grab a ball that has handles on it, carry it over to an elevated basket, and throw it through. All while staying on the horse. Really. Go to Argentina if you don't believe me—it's their national sport.

ORIGINALLY, PATO WAS NOT PLAYED WITH A BALL, BUT WITH A DUCK IN A BASKET. A DUCK! IN A BASKET!

48 Joust.

You ride a horse carrying a lance (read: a large spear), and gallop full-tilt in one direction. Someone else on a horse, who also has a spear, gallops at you. You try to knock the other person off his or her horse, while the other rider tries to do the same to you. If you do this, you deserve whatever happens to you. You'll probably have to join a Renaissance Fair or the Society for Creative Anachronism to participate.

49 Ride an elephant.

☠ ☠ ☠ ☠

The elephant is the largest land animal on Earth. You don't even come close.

MANY JURISDICTIONS ARE BANNING ELEPHANT RIDES AT PARKS, ZOOS, AND CIRCUSES TO PREVENT INJURIES AND/OR DEATHS CAUSED BY RAMPAGING ELEPHANTS.

50 Ride a mechanical bull.

☠ ☠ ☠

This has all the appeal of riding a real bull outdoors, with the added fun of being able to collide with a wall, the ceiling, drunken onlookers wearing big belt buckles, some tables, various glass objects, and a floor that's much harder than a pasture.

51 Ride an ostrich.

☠ ☠ ☠

Why would you want to ride a bird? That's silly. And the ostrich knows it's silly. The ostrich will be glad to let you know how silly it is. According to North Dakota State University, an adult ostrich can kick with 500 pounds of pressure per square inch. Several sources suggest that one person per year, from 1997 to 2000, was killed by ostriches. How silly would you feel if you were killed by an ostrich?

52 Drive a dogsled.

☠ ☠

It's a sled, in the snow, pulled by a pack of dogs. Balance counts.

53 Race a dogsled.

☠ ☠ ☠

It's dogsleds, all trying to beat each other to the finish line. The mass start is the most fascinating aspect of this race, as the dogs would much rather meet the other dogs, run around, play—pretty much do anything other than drag your sorry ass toward the finish line.

54 Ride a BMX bike.

☠ ☠

It stands for "bicycle motocross," in case you were wondering. Usually a small, sturdy, lightweight frame, with heavy, ridged tires, for purposes of going off-road and doing tricks. People over the age of thirty need not apply.

Take employment as a bike messenger in a metropolitan area.

☠☠☠☠

Potholes. Traffic. Pedestrians. Curbs. Many, many ways to die. And speed is your trade. Good luck.

Ride a bicycle across the United States.

☠☠☠☠☠

Just think of the valuable exercise this will afford you! Think of the grandeur of the scenery!

THINK OF THE COMPLETE AND UTTER EXHAUSTION YOU WILL FACE EACH NIGHT.

Do a triathlon.

☠☠☠

This was one of those "sports" invented by those who didn't find one particular event enough of a challenge. A race comprised of one leg of swimming, one of biking, and a run (usually in that order), this is pure punishment. The participant must go from one phase to the next, while the time in transit is counted right along with the time of each event.

58 Swim with sharks.

☠☠☠☠☠

Millions of years of evolution have not changed this animal; it is perfectly suited to hunt and kill in its environment. According to the Florida Museum of Natural History's International Shark Attack File, the number of shark attacks is steadily increasing each decade. According to the file, though, this is only because of an increase in the number of people getting close to sharks. Not that this will comfort you in any way if you end up with a three-tiered chomp on your abdomen.

59 Swim with dolphins.

☠

Awww . . . aren't they cute? Don't you just love those funny little clicking-whistling noises they make? They're just so sweet on TV and in the movies, aren't they? They're wild animals. Get over it. They're not there for your amusement, and they don't like you.

60 Swim with jellyfish.

☠☠☠

We all know they sting, and that their sting hurts in a nasty, severe way. But did you know they swarm? The little bastards get together in clusters of hundreds, all just floating serenely, waiting for some unwary swimmer to hit them and get stung repeatedly. Ugly.

61 Learn to scuba-dive.

☠☠

Breathing underwater is surreal in a very concrete way. You're underwater, and you're breathing. This makes no sense. But this is as close to freefall as us nonastronauts will get. Get information from the international instruction entities before signing up for any scuba school: NAUI (*www.naui.com*) and PADI (*www.padi.com*).

62 Scuba in a cave.

☠☠☠

Known as "cave diving," this combines the thrill of going both underwater and underground. What better way to fulfill your claustrophobia quota for the rest of your natural life? Be sure to bring some light sources; it's doubly dark down there.

63 Get punched in the face, at least once.

☠ ☠ ☠

We don't let just anyone come close to our face—it is uncomfortable. Up close and personal, you can smell someone's breath, see all the little faults, and there's the constant threat that they will kiss you. So getting punched in the face is a miserable experience; it drops everything you are to a simple common denominator: "I just got punched in the face."

A PUNCH IN THE FACE CAUSES A LOT MORE DAMAGE IN REAL LIFE THAN IN THE MOVIES—TO BOTH THE PUNCHER AND THE PUNCHEE.

64 Learn a martial art.

☠ ☠ ☠

Martial arts, unlike other contact sports, promise the supposition that if you're good, really good, you won't have to get hit. Don't believe it—nobody's that good. Bruce Lee wasn't that good. And you're not Bruce Lee.

65 Fight someone in a competition.

You get the great fun of being punched (and kicked) in the head and body, with the additional bonus of getting to be humiliated in front of an audience.

66 Fight someone obviously far more skilled than you.

Okay, that punch you see coming, that's the easy one; that one is just going to snap your head backwards, bend your neck a little, give you that sharp slapping pain. The tough one is the one they tell you about when you find yourself on the mat.

67 Try fencing.

☠☠

Sure, the end of the foil (that stabby thing? that's a foil, or saber, or an épée) is blunted; you can't really poke through anything (like, say, skin) with the tip. Tell that to your eye when it comes whipping past your face. Your reflexes say "go," when you're supposed to be doing something about it . . . like fighting back.

68 Play jai alai.

☠☠☠☠☠+

Sure, the ball is only a quarter pound, but it's still going to leave a mark. Imagine getting hit by a half-brick thrown from a speeding motorcycle. Which is kinda funny, when you think about it. But not so funny when it's a jai alai pelota hurled by some crazed Basque. Although, it's a lot of fun to say "jai alai" and "pelota." And "Basque."

ONE PHRASE TO REMEMBER ABOUT JAI ALAI: "FASTEST-MOVING BALL IN SPORTS." WE'RE TALKING 180 MILES PER HOUR.

69 Try water-skiing.

This is a special technique, devised by early-twentieth-century Americans, with which to force as much water into your lungs as possible, in the shortest conceivable length of time. Want that lake drained? Hire some water-skiers. If you go face-first into the water, that water is going into your face at the speed the boat was traveling when you hit the surface—and you have holes in your face.

THE WATER, AS WATER DOES, WILL LOOK FOR THE PATH OF LEAST RESISTANCE WHEN YOU'RE WATER-SKIING. THAT'S THE HOLES IN YOUR FACE.

70 Luge.

☠ ☠ ☠ ☠

Start with a bobsled. Take away the camaraderie offered by cramming next to someone of the same gender while wearing polyurethane winter speed suits. Take away the comfort of sitting like a normal human being. Take away the sides and front end of the vehicle. What you're left with is luge.

Street luge.

Laying on your back, on a composite-metal frame, speeding feet-first down a hilly road, your head is propped up so you can look out over your toes at what's coming. You're inches from the concrete. You can—theoretically—steer. In the words of my friend Andrew Harley: "There's a game definitely invented when Mom wasn't home." It started in Southern California, of course. It's now worldwide, with competitions on this continent, Europe, and Africa.

Play Hornussen.

Supposedly, this Swiss sport involves a projectile moving at speeds above 150 miles per hour. A bizarre combination of golf and tennis, hornussen involves two competing teams that try to block each other's missiles, which are launched with a whiplike club. The further your "nouss" (the pucklike projectile) travels, the more points you get . . . but your opponents are allowed to knock it down mid-flight, using big paddles that look like signs you'd see protesters carrying. Bizarre. Oh—and you have to go to Switzerland to play.

73 Launch an arrow using a bow.

☠ ☠

A big, honking compound bow. Feel that sharp, slapping sting on your forearm? That's 'cause you didn't bend your elbow enough. The bow is probably the only self-correcting weapon that isn't fatal.

74 Fire a bolt using a crossbow.

☠

All of the benefits of a bow, with none of the drawbacks. So simple, even a child can put a projectile through the wall of a house. These can be cocked with a lever mechanism, making them easier to draw, and are fired by pulling a trigger, making it possible to hold your aim indefinitely. Also, it's aimed like longarm, with the bow horizontal, allowing an easier line of sight, and good placement for a scope.

75 Go hang-gliding off a cliff.

☠ ☠ ☠ ☠

Now that we, as a race, have finally accomplished the goal of creating a mechanism whereby we can take to the air, traversing the atmosphere, in a safe, reliable manner, why not go for it? A hang glider is a fabric wing, with straps (or a chassis, depending on the type) to secure the human pilot below it. The pilot steers either by shifting body weight or by using controls on the wing itself (again, depending on the type of hang glider).

DO YOU THINK IT WOULD BE A GOOD IDEA TO TIE YOURSELF TO A KITE AND JUMP OFF SOMETHING—HIGH?

Try paragliding.

☠ ☠ ☠

This is not parasailing. Parasailing has you tethered to a motorboat, like a ridiculous human kite. Paragliding, on the other hand, is a means of actually propelling yourself through the sky, using only a running start, the wind currents, and aeronautics to move you, like a ridiculous human kite. It's very similar to hang-gliding, except that the wing is comprised of a series of fabric cells, instead of a rigid wing. You may want to get a little training before you try something like this.

77 Pilot a kayak.

☠☠☠

So canoeing is too easy, you say? Rafting just doesn't have that thrill of a rugged individual sport? Try kayaking. You're right-side up—then you're upside down. You're fighting a body of water of some kind, and you're all on your own.

78 Sail a small (less than three-person) sailboat.

☠☠

There are all sorts of hooks and pulleys and big pieces of cloth, and you have to make them all work together. If you can pull this off, you are able to replicate one of the oldest forms of locomotion in human history, traveling the way our distant ancestors did.

WHY YOU'D WANT TO BOTHER WITH A DINKY SAILBOAT, WHEN CIGARETTE BOATS ARE AVAILABLE, IS BEYOND ME.

79 Sail a yacht.

☠☠☠

One of those big mothers. On the open ocean. Look out for pirates and sea monsters and stuff.

80 Wrestle an alligator.

☠☠☠☠☠

Here's a giant reptile, about as unevolved as a shark (no need to evolve when you're an almost perfectly designed predator). Isn't it a cool giant reptile? Let's grab it and fight with it, mano a mano. Because, you know, we're equipped with these wicked fingernails and massive muscles. . . . Oh, wait. There are plenty of places in Florida (and nearby states) where you can go see this—but none that will let you, the tourist, try it. The liability is just too great.

81 Wrestle a bear.

☠☠☠☠☠

Here's the most formidable, omnivorous mammal in the world. According to several news sources, bear wrestling is illegal in twenty states. Before attempting, find out if it's permissible in your locale. If it is, still avoid this.

82 Attempt extreme ironing.

☠☠☠☠

From the Web site of the Extreme Ironing Bureau (*www.extremeironing.com*): "The sport that is 'extreme ironing' is an outdoor activity that combines the danger and excitement of an 'extreme' sport with the satisfaction of a well pressed shirt." Ironers have ironed on top of mountains, under bogs, and on nude beaches. Because, even when you're doing something extremely dangerous, it's important to be well-pressed. Supposedly, there's some dude ironing underwater in Madagascar. Righteous.

83 Participate in a rodeo.

☠☠☠☠

This is an activity that involves kicking farm critters with metal spikes worn on your heels, in order to infuriate them.

IF YOU EVER JUMPED ON MY BACK, JABBED SPURS INTO MY SIDE, AND TRIED TO MAKE ME DO SOMETHING, I'D BE PRETTY PISSED OFF, TOO.

84 Fight a bull.

☠ ☠ ☠ ☠

Sword? Check. Cape? Check. Shiny pants? Check. Okay, you're now well armed to go up against a ton of vicious animal flesh. But in the traditional form, you can't just go do that—no, you have to get eight of your friends to poke and harass the poor creature first, and weaken it to the point where you really don't have to do much work yourself. I root for the bull.

85 Attempt bull riding.

☠ ☠ ☠ ☠

A rodeo event wherein you, the rider, get on a large male bovine and try to remain there for eight seconds, holding on with only one hand. This could have quite easily been started as a cowboy-fraternity initiation prank.

86 Do a logroll.

Supposedly, this comes from the dated practice of sending logs downriver to the sawmill. The lumberjacks had to ride the logs on the water, to assist in preventing logjams. (See the Paul Newman movie *Sometimes a Great Notion*, based on the excellent book by Ken Kesey, if you can find a copy.) You're standing on a log, which is floating in the water. There is also an opponent standing on the log. You both try to spin the log as it floats, with the objective of getting the other person to fall.

WARNING: LOGROLLING COULD HAVE AN ADVERSE EFFECT ON YOUR SEX LIFE.

87 Go deep-sea fishing.

A macho goofball author once wrote a book all about an old guy who went and did this, and had a rotten time. I kind of think that's fairly accurate. You: sit in a boat, in a comfy chair, with as many beers as you'd like, and a high-tech rod and reel designed specifically to yank game fish out of the ocean. The fish: gets snagged in the mouth by a hook and fights for its life. Gosh, you're impressive. Hang that thing on your wall.

88 Try your hand at commercial fishing.

☠ ☠ ☠ ☠ ☠

There are heavy ropes, cold seas, harsh conditions, giant storms, pirates, and big-ass fish ready to knock you overboard into turbulent water. Let's hope there's good money in it, because, according to the federal Centers for Disease Control (which tracks stuff like this), Alaskan commercial fishing resulted in 28 times more occupational deaths than the U.S. average, as of the turn of the twenty-first century. National average: 4.4 deaths per 100,000 workers each year; Alaskan commercial fishers: 124 deaths per 100,000 workers.

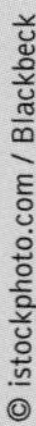

89 Go spearfishing.

☠ ☠ ☠

A lot more complicated than regular fishing: this is just you, a pointy stick, and the free-roaming fish (well, as free-roaming as fish get—they gotta stay in the water, of course). You have to be able to nail a moving creature, taking into account the diffraction of reflected light from water to air, just by jabbing quickly. Tough.

90 Go ice-fishing.

☠ ☠ ☠

Find a body of water that has frozen over (one that has fish in it, preferably). Cut a hole in the ice. Drop your fishing line down into the water. Sit and wait until you catch a fish. I think this is mostly about drinking beer.

#90

91 Go crabbing.

☠ ☠ ☠

Trying to harvest crabs is not a simple, sedentary pursuit, like some other types of fishing. Crabs are scuttling, frisky things, with pincers designed to, well, pinch. They will let you know that they don't like being harvested in the manner best suited to their species. Most crabbing is done via the use of traps; cagelike boxes of metal or wood, which allow the crabs to walk right in and sample whatever bait you've placed inside. You drop your trap down into the water, letting it sink to the bottom. A buoy attached to a line on the trap lets you know where you left it. You go back after a while and pull the thing back up. Maybe there's crabs inside, maybe there aren't.

CHECK ALL LOCAL LAWS BEFORE ATTEMPTING TO CRAB—DIFFERENT PLACES HAVE WIDELY VARYING RULES.

92 Learn to throw a bladed tool of some kind.

☠

There are plenty of things designed specifically for throwing, and many of them are pointed or edged. There are special throwing knives, throwing axes, and the ever-popular "throwing stars," or shuriken, from martial arts movies. They are also pretty simple to use, if you've got some patience. You can set up a training area anywhere you want: your bedroom, the basement, outside. Anywhere with enough distance to throw something accurately (say, ten yards, tops). Make sure you have a good backstop so that you're not throwing sharp things past your target; a nice, wide, wooden tabletop, hefted vertically, is a good choice. And try not to scare the neighbors.

93 Throw a spear/javelin.

☠ ☠

It looks as if it would be easy, because gravity's doing most of the work, right? Actually hitting something you're aiming at, or even getting a considerable distance, though, is a bit more tricky. You need a nice, long, empty area to practice this, the size of a public park or playing field—but both those places discourage people from throwing pointy objects up in the air, because the pointy objects have to come down sometime. Which seems reasonable.

94 Walk on stilts.

☠ ☠

It's spooky, teetering up so high, with nothing to support you but your own treasonous sense of balance. But if you have the patience to learn this, just think: you can always make a practice of scaring small children by being that person who dresses up for the parade and ambles along, staring down at people and waving.

95 Throw a bolas.

☠ ☠ ☠

Here's a dandy little tool that can quite easily kill the wielder just as readily as function properly. Made of strips of leather or rope with heavy weights on the end, the bolas is used primarily in South America to trip large animals. It's thrown by gauchos. So, if nothing else comes of the experience, you get to use the word *gaucho* quite often, which is a big bonus. You might not want to try this when you're having an "off" day. For target practice, you'll want to find something upright and fairly narrow, like a young tree or fencepost.

BOLAS AREN'T TOO GOOD OVER LONG DISTANCES, THOUGH—STAY WITHIN TWENTY YARDS.

96 Crack a bullwhip.

It's really not as hard to crack a bullwhip as you might think. Of course, controlling where the thing cracks, and what it does before and after the crack, is something else entirely. And that nifty stuff they do with whips, in movies? Like having the whip twist around a beam so that the wielder can swing from one place to another, or grab a person's limb, or whatever? Not real likely.

97 Swing on a rope from one place to another.

Of course, it is traditional to give full voice to a Tarzan-like yodel as you're traversing space. For which you receive style points. You may have to set this up on your own property, with the rope attached to a house or tree.

98 Roll down a hill in a Zorb.

☠

Ever have a hamster? Okay, ever see a hamster? You know those little plastic balls they roll around in? Well, now somebody makes giant ones, suitable for people, surrounded by soft plastic air cushions. So if you've ever wanted to be a hamster, or just feel like a hamster, this is the thing for you.

FOR FURTHER ZORB-ROLLING INSPIRATION, YOU CAN WATCH RERUNS OF *THE PRISONER*.

99 Hunt a falcon.

☠☠☠

No, I don't mean go out with a shotgun and stalk a bird of prey; I mean you should try being a falconer. Getting a recalcitrant, obstinate, independent animal like a raptor to do your bidding is quite a challenge—and don't romanticize the activity; the birds, while graceful and cool to look at, are smelly, mean, filthy, and damned dangerous. Plus, cutting up various rodents and game birds to feed the hunters is a nasty, unpleasant business.

100 Fire a handgun.

☠ ☠

What most folks won't tell you, whether they're antigun or not, is that a pistol feels good in your hand. It was designed specifically to fit in your palm and be squeezed. Shooting at something and hitting it, well, that feels fantastic. Try shooting solid targets—bottles and cans. There is something far more satisfying about making something jump or shatter, as opposed to putting tiny little holes in a piece of paper. Be sure you have plenty of room for this—a certified shooting range is best. Know the parameters of your gun and ammo.

101 Fire a rifle.

☠ ☠

This is a lot trickier than a handgun. A rifle is supposed to fit snugly in your arms. It should rest comfortably perched in the crook of your shoulder. Human bodies, however, vary a lot more, and in wildly more ways, than human hands; unless you have a firearm custom-tailored to your body specifications, it's never going to feel as simply correct as a pistol. It's a lot more accurate, though.

A SIMPLE .22 ROUND CAN TRAVERSE A MILE OVER LAND, AND TWO MILES OVER WATER (YES, THEY CAN SKIP). BE SURE YOU HAVE ENOUGH OPEN AREA, OR A GREAT BACKSTOP.

102 Fire a shotgun at trap clays.

This activity was supposedly designed to simulate the experience of hunting game birds. Instead of birds, the participant fires a series of quick shotgun blasts at small, round, clay targets. There's a single launching point (a "house") that throws the small disks out ahead of the shooter's position, at varying angles and trajectories. Many people think that a shotgun is some magic destructive paintbrush that will destroy anything in the vicinity of where it's pointing when fired. Not so—the shot pattern of a group of pellets is actually fairly small—and hitting a fist-sized target flying away from you at a good clip is not nearly as easy as you might think.

103 Play racquetball.

☠ ☠

It's all about speed, motion, and angles. You have to have some serious stamina for this, and a knowledge of rudimentary physics. That ball is small, hard, and made of rubber, and stings if it hits you. Head shots are bad, but exposed skin is even worse—the welts can remain for weeks.

104 Fire an automatic weapon, on automatic.

☠ ☠

Movies and television have led the casual viewer to believe that this technique is an easy way of obliterating whatever you want to destroy. Not so. It's almost impossible to aim a weapon on full auto; the muzzle tends to rise and drift as the repetitive blowback hammers at your grip. But man—what a rush.

105 Skip rope.

☠ ☠ ☠

Oh, yeah—you think it looks easy, right? Think maybe it's a pastime for little kids? So go on, show us what you've got. This takes not just agility and timing, but stamina, too. Why do you think so many boxers do this? That's right.

IF YOU THINK SKIPPING ROPE IS STILL TOO SIMPLE, TRY THE ARMS-CROSSED STROKE, OR TRY DOING IT WITH ANKLE WEIGHTS.

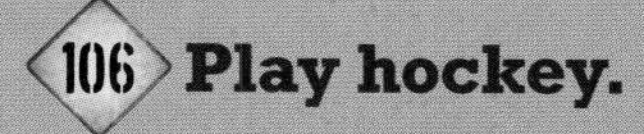

106 Play hockey.

☠ ☠ ☠ ☠

Ice is not a natural supporter of human life. It saps the strength and energy of wimpy warm-blooded bodies with no fur. So somebody had the bright idea to put a semicontact game on top of the stuff. Go figure.

Run with a herd of bulls.

☠☠☠

You see that bull? Yeah, that one. Doesn't look real fast, does it? Doesn't seem like it's anything other than a male cow, right? Just lying there, chewing on some grass, it looks pretty sedentary. Oh—didn't they mention? Bulls can hit running speeds close to that of a horse—right around 45 miles per hour. The fastest Olympic runner can do 10.2 meters per second, which equals roughly 27 miles per hour. So, uh . . . what were you thinking?

RUNNING WITH BULLS IS ONE OF THOSE REALLY STUPID THINGS YOU ONLY DO SO YOU CAN SAY YOU DID IT. I DID IT.

Raft a white-water river.

☠ – ☠☠☠☠, depending on conditions

You go up and down, side to side, splashing, flailing, twisting, and turning. This is a fantastic experience—and one with the peril of possibly drowning.

109 Throw a boomerang.

☠ ☠

Theoretically, if you do it correctly, it will come back to you. Why you'd want a heavy, thin piece of hardwood flying at your body is another story.

110 Play football.

☠ – ☠ ☠ ☠ ☠ ☠, depending on conditions

There are many varieties of this game, from fun-with-the-fam-on-the-lawn-two-hand-touch, to Corporate Grudge Flag, to the ol' fashioned, brain-rattling tackle.

111 Try to pole vault.

☠ ☠ ☠

Physics plays a significant role in this activity. Work on your upper-body strength, and get a damned good coach before attempting this. Really.

Play water polo.

☠ ☠

This is like hockey, but actually in the water. So now you can add drowning to the possible implications. Nifty.

Play underwater hockey.

☠ ☠ ☠

Okay, now you're under the water. The stamina required for this activity outstrips just about everything else. You get a small stick, about two hand-spans long, which you use to push a weighted puck across the bottom of the pool. The opposing team tries to push the puck in the other direction. Fun, but very, very difficult.

PLAYING UNDERWATER HOCKEY IS QUITE POSSIBLY THE MOST BRUTAL WAY TO PUNISH YOUR LUNGS AND INNER EAR.

Play polo.

☠ ☠ ☠

Hockey on horses. Lots of horses. Really fast horses. And really long mallets. With a big-ass plastic ball that soars at head-height.

115 Play soccer with Europeans.

☠ ☠ ☠

This is not fun for them. This is not sport. This is religion. Anyone who wasn't sleeping through history class in high school remembers what religious Europeans did when they decided they wanted a chunk of Middle Eastern desert for themselves. Same kind of thing. It will get bloody.

116 Play slamball.

☠ ☠

Because, y'know, basketball just wasn't intense enough. So they added some trampolines and plastic walls, and took away some of the rules.

117 Roller-skate.

☠

Some balance is involved. Granted, it's pretty easy once you get the hang of it, but some people never quite accomplish even that.

118 Play roller derby.

☠ ☠ ☠

You thought this had fled with the 1970s, didn't ya? Well, it did . . . but it keeps trying to spring up again, like a weed. And, admittedly, the fascination is largely attributed to that portion of the brain that also enjoys women-in-prison movies. Two teams of five female players each skate counter-clockwise around an oval track. Yes.

119 Participate in building a human pyramid.

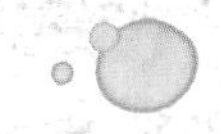

☠

Well, duh—obviously, it's better to be as close to the top as possible. Of course, then you have farther to fall. . . .

120 Try sculling.

☠ ☠

Actually, sculling is a subset of the activity entitled "sport rowing," and is the type with two oars (sweep-oar rowing has the participant wielding just one oar). But it's much more fun to say "sculling" than "sport rowing," even though it's much more pretentious.

IF I HAD TO SCULL, I'D RATHER BE THE COXSWAIN, THE PERSON SITTING IN THE FRONT OF THE BOAT, YELLING AT THE ROWERS TO ROW HARDER.

121 Engage in a hearty round of dodgeball.

☠☠–☠☠☠☠☠, depending on circumstances

Mostly, in this country, dodgeball is played by prepubescent children whose bodies are comprised mostly of spongy cartilage and mucus; it is for this reason that there are so few dodgeball-related permanent injuries and disfigurements in the medical texts. To play as an adult, well, that's bordering on lunacy. Some colleges have formed amateur dodgeball leagues, so if you want to play, you might want to matriculate at Michigan State University, Ohio State, the University of Kentucky, Lesley College, or the Art Institute of Boston. There are rumors of at least one grudge match played between Harvard and MIT.

IF YOU'RE OUT OF COLLEGE, CHECK OUT THE NATIONAL AMATEUR DODGEBALL ASSOCIATION, AT *WWW.DODGEBALLUSA.COM.*

122 Take part in a cardboard regatta.

☠☠

Maybe you find sailing and sculling fun but tame. . . . Why not make your own watercraft out of recyclable paper products? This was someone's nifty idea, and, unfortunately, it never died with that person. So now, supposedly, there are hordes of people across the country who build and propel their own corrugated-cardboard boats. Really.

123 Play paintball.

☠☠

There's nothing quite as much fun as shooting your friends. And, while not truly harmful, getting nailed by one of those suckers hurts. Really and truly. So try to remember all the minor slights and insults your friends have caused you over the years, use that for motivation, and get cracking. There are several varieties of games you can play, including versions of "Capture the Flag" and "Tag." Sometimes, though, it's just more fun to re-enact a classical European duel of honor.

124 Enter a demolition derby.

☠☠☠

Only in a nation as absurdly oversupplied with technological goodness as our own could such a pastime develop naturally. Here's the deal: a bunch of people take a bunch of cars into an arena. The drivers bash the other people's cars with their own. The last driver with a drivable (moving) car wins. I have heard that it is best to go in reverse during this type of competition, as most vehicles have an engine in the front, and you want to avoid disabling the engine.

SOCIAL THINGS Let's face it: All our real fears—or most of the serious ones, at any rate—have to do with how we deal with other people. Nothing is as intimidating as our interactions, be they with strangers, friends, family, colleagues, or loved ones. Where do we rank in the eyes of others? How are we supposed to behave? Will we look like idiots, and embarrass ourselves? Even the athletic stuff is compounded by the social aspect—losing a game is bad, but losing it in front of other people, or knowing that other people will hear of the loss, is excruciating.

Take a loud contrary viewpoint in a roomful of people dedicated to the thing you're attacking.

This is particularly intriguing when it involves politics, religion, or sex. Even more so when it includes all three. For instance, you might want to assert that you think Buddha would be against any laws that prohibit sodomy, or that the pope would sanction equal opportunity quotas for prostitutes.

126 Teach a high school class.

Find a teacher in your community who welcomes guest lecturers, preferably on a topic with which you're familiar. Prepare a presentation. Go in and try to make the little monsters learn something. This is the most difficult audience you will ever face: they don't think you're cool and they don't like what you're talking about.

REMEMBER: HIGH-SCHOOLERS ARE ONLY THERE BECAUSE THE LAW SAYS THEY HAVE TO BE.

127 Make a public presentation of some sort. If you're really brave, do it in front of your peers, friends, and relatives.

There are no harsher critics than somebody who knows you intimately—they'll be glad to tell you how much you sucked.

128 Write a letter of protest.

☠☠

Really use your personal freedom, and stand up for what you believe in. Or sit down, rather—it's easier to write or type while seated. Let someone know how you feel, and how you think that whatever that person did (or didn't do) was/is wrong. Put your actual name on it—anonymous letters of protest are for wimps.

129 Take part in a prank that is nothing less than childishly foolish.

☠☠

Let's say that you make a mannequin out of an old pair of Levi's and a flannel shirt stuffed with straw, and you pop on a head made from a car-wash sponge mitten. Maybe even pour ketchup over his mitten head, like he's suffered a grievous trauma. And then let's just say you prop him out on a suburban road, sitting atop a large hunk of firewood, with his legs crossed, in a graceful manner, like he's drinking a martini and smoking a cigarette. Let's say you do this late on Halloween night. At, like, 11 P.M. or so. You'd obviously hide in the bushes on the side of the road, right? I mean, you'd wait to watch some car drive along and see this dude sitting there, and you'd want to see what they'd do. What would you do if that first car were a squad car?

Run from the cops.

☠ ☠ ☠

Maybe you aren't doing anything bad, per se. Not even really all that illegal. Like maybe underage drinking. And maybe you're just walking along the railroad tracks, headed home. But when you see that cop, the adrenaline kicks in and you bolt for cover.

Get arrested.

☠ ☠ ☠ ☠

Most of the time, our mass media teaches us that cops are to be trusted—that they might have personal foibles, but they're basically good people. Many of our parents, teachers, and other trusted adults tell us this when we're growing up, too. And we learn to assume that cops will be trustworthy and fair. When you end up with your hands cuffed behind you, sitting in the back of that squad car, try to remember those things: The experience casts those beliefs into a stark light.

DON'T SLIDE YOUR CUFFS UNDER YOUR LEGS, SO THAT YOU CAN SIT COMFORTABLY WITH THE CUFFS IN YOUR LAP—COPS DON'T LIKE THAT.

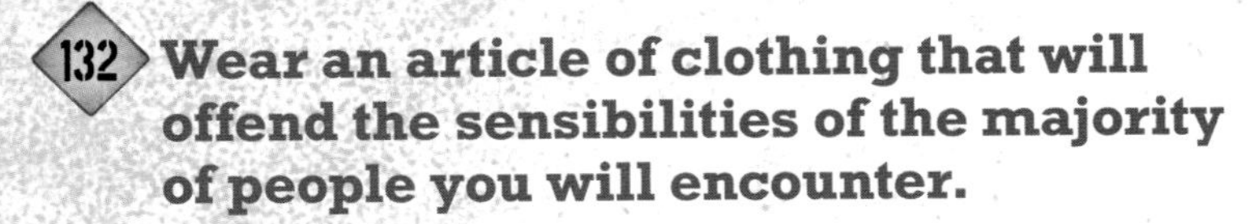

132 Wear an article of clothing that will offend the sensibilities of the majority of people you will encounter.

☠

There are entire companies dedicated to selling merchandise to accomplish this. Teenagers do it constantly. Of course, teens are also stupid enough to say stuff like, "Hey, dude, don't judge me by what I wear," when they specifically selected a given piece of apparel for the express purpose of looking different from everybody else.

DON A SHIRT TITLED "OFFICIAL BREAST INSPECTOR" BEFORE ATTENDING A WOMEN'S RIGHTS CONFERENCE. YOU GET THE IDEA.

133 Bring a pet to a place that is completely inappropriate or prohibited.

☠ ☠ ☠

Like, say, a dog in an institution of higher learning. Or a rat in a restaurant. Or a reptile wherever. Doing something daring is usually pretty risky, but it's you taking the risk, and you can control yourself to a great extent. You'll never know how an animal, however, will react. Much more risky.

134 Streak.

☠

There is something to be said for moving about without clothing; it's liberating, in the sense that you become truly free of restraint. Restraint of clothing, that is. You also become a lot more susceptible to the elements. Hey, it's your liberation—do with it what you will. Reports of streaking go as far back as 1970 at Princeton University, and 1972 at Notre Dame. Many colleges have seen this fad come and go. And come. And go.

135 Tell a lie.

☠ – ☠ ☠ ☠ ☠ ☠, depending on conditions

You don't want to make a habit of this; it's much harder to keep track of lies than the truth, and it's quite possible they will convene in an awkward manner and trip you up. So select specific instances where a big, beautiful lie will do the trick, and reserve the practice for those occasions.

136 Visit a prison.

☠☠☠

This is the real deal. A prison seems surreal, because it is probably the only place on the planet specifically designed to diminish every natural urge, need, and craving of the human spirit. It looks like it, too. If you feel totally despondent and ill-at-ease while walking around, that was the intent.

137 Escape from a prison.

☠☠☠☠☠

This can involve a complex plan involving twine, the patrol schedule, a tunnel, and a small aerial vehicle made from styrofoam cups and rubber bands, or it can be a straightforward matter of running off from a work detail. Your choice. There are plenty of types of prisons, too. . . . High school might reasonably be considered a prison, as can many relationships.

138 Interview a killer.

☠ ☠ ☠

All sorts of people have actually killed another person: soldiers, cops, security personnel, homeowners who act in self-defense, etc. But for real daring, you have to sit down and have a conversation with a murderer. This is not easy, as murderers are necessarily creepy. That's part of the reason they're murderers.

139 Attend a rave.

☠ ☠

You know, those crazy, quasi-legal gatherings involving heavy use of Ecstasy and lots of ultraviolet lighting. A rave, dude. For, like, techno music and glow lights. And to appease that adolescent angst you never really kicked.

SUPPOSEDLY, THERE'S A WAY TO FIND THESE OFT-ILLICIT GATHERINGS BY FOLLOWING CODES FOUND IN YOUR LOCAL NEWSPAPER, BUT DAMNED IF I CAN FIGURE IT OUT.

Crash a party.

☠

Sometimes you can accomplish this completely by accident. You've wandered into a club/restaurant/meeting place, and there are people gathered there, drinking, laughing, having a generally good time. You can blend right in.

JUST DON'T BRING DOWN THE FUN—THAT'S THE ONLY RULE FOR ATTENDING A PARTY WHEN YOU WEREN'T INVITED.

Join the military.

☠ ☠ ☠

Doesn't have to be active duty; it can be reserve or guard. But active duty is really jumping in with both feet. For details, contact your local recruiter.

© istockphoto.com / imagesunlimiteduk

142 Do a ride-along with the police department.

Contact your local law enforcement department for scheduling. This is prurient voyeurism at its utmost; nothing else quite lets you rub your shoulders gently up against the grit—without getting any on yourself, of course. You have no reason for being there. You should probably be more honest with yourself and go watch some porn instead.

143 Join a volunteer fire department.

☠ – ☠☠☠☠, depending on duties performed

There is probably nothing nobler than running into a burning building to save people trapped inside. If you can't swing that, the fire department probably still needs people to do paperwork, sweep up the place, and answer the phone. The nobility is only somewhat diminished for these support duties.

144 Try to save someone's life.

☠☠ – ☠☠☠☠☠, depending on circumstances

For something involving pure coincidence, there are a surprising number of opportunities available; people are constantly having heart seizures, choking, falling, or drowning. You might want to learn CPR, lifeguard swimming, some first aid, and the Heimlich. Suggestion: After intervening in a possibly deadly situation, get away as soon as possible. It's quite possible to hurt someone while saving them, and people have a really weird sense of gratitude . . . which often involves litigation.

145 Intervene to prevent a crime.

☠☠☠☠

If more citizens just acted to uphold the law, there would probably be a lot less crime. Of course, there would probably be many more dead would-be heroes, too.

146 Make a citizen's arrest.

☠☠☠☠☠

Every state in the Union has provisions for everyday people to nab lawbreakers. Try to bear this in mind, however: Professional law enforcement officials are not subject, as individuals, to many civil and criminal liabilities that you, as a common citizen, may be subject to, even if you're absolutely correct in making an arrest.

NOBODY, BUT NOBODY, WILL ENCOURAGE YOU TO MAKE A CITIZEN'S ARREST—INCLUDING ME.

147 Cook a meal for twelve or more people.

☠☠

Even if you can cook, you're really looking at something daunting here. . . . It's not just a matter of scaling up your normal recipes; the kind of volume required doesn't allow for that kind of easy modification.

WARNING: COOKING FOR A GROUP WILL PUSH YOU TO YOUR LIMITS, TAKING UP ALL YOUR COUNTER SPACE, EVERY POT AND PAN, AND THE ENTIRETY OF YOUR FRIDGE.

148 Participate in a scavenger hunt.

☠ – ☠☠☠☠, depending on circumstances

Collect things. Race around. Get goofy with friends. Depending on complexity and duration, scavenger hunts can be fairly easy or damned difficult. They're almost always fun.

149 Sit in the front row at a rock concert.

☠☠

Performers, when performing, do a lot of crazy things. You might catch a piece of concert memorabilia thrown by a performer, or get chosen to join the act onstage, or just get hit with a rock star's sweat. Cool.

150 Jump into a mosh pit.

☠☠☠

This is a concert-going practice invented by numbskulled teens. Instead of just listening to the music, or dancing, or holding up a cigarette lighter, these imbeciles enjoy the performance by slamming their bodies into each other. Maybe because they're too clumsy to dance.

151 Attend a punk concert.

☠ ☠ ☠

A punk concert is like a giant mosh pit. This is difficult to do, because there really aren't any punk bands left anymore. You could probably attend a punk cover band concert, which might be a bit like the same thing. For modern quasi-punk, you might want to catch a Leftover Crack show. I won't be there.

152 Lick a flagpole in winter.

☠ ☠ ☠

I triple-dog dare you. This is an absolute must, an homage to both the playground and Jean Shepherd, creator of the classic film, *A Christmas Story*, which features a flagpole-licking scene. Too good.

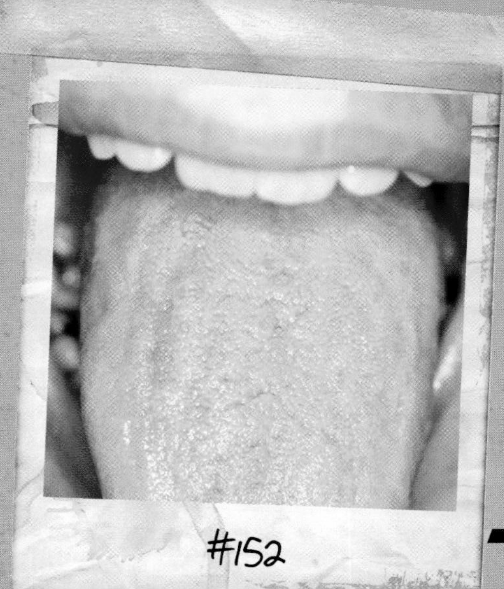

Attend a family reunion.

Not that you really like any of those people. . . . But for a freak of genetics and gestation, you wouldn't even know some of them. But they are your family, and always good for a laugh or two, so give it a whirl.

REMEMBER: YOU CAN ALWAYS LEAVE FAMILY REUNIONS EARLY.

Attend a high school reunion.

Let's be perfectly frank: Regardless of the comments and arguments made by those who purport to speak with authority, life is just like high school. High school is basically a microcosm of the entirety of human existence, sad as that may be. So don't you really want to see how everyone turned out? Don't you want them to see how you turned out?

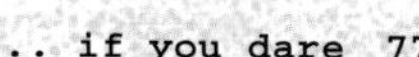

155 Attend a high school reunion and stay sober.

☠☠☠

Facing this kind of trauma without the benefit of some anesthesia or other is the zenith of folly.

156 Act as the witness to an accident.

☠☠

Somebody got wrapped up, and you watched it happen. It is now your civic duty to stand around and wait for the authorities to take statements. This really benefits those involved (well, those who weren't negligently responsible, of course), and helps them get their insurance claims in a timely and proper manner. Hey—wouldn't you want someone to help out if you were in an accident . . . if it wasn't your fault?

AS A WITNESS, BE PREPARED TO EXERCISE YOUR PATIENCE. THE POLICE TEND TO OPERATE ON THEIR OWN SCHEDULE.

157 Provide first aid to an accident victim.

☠ ☠ ☠

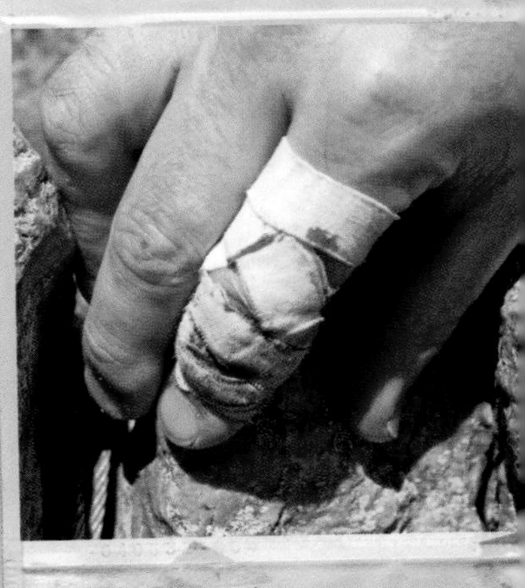

Someone's hurt, and you can do something about it. So you should. Even if you're not a doctor, nurse, or paramedic, and even if you've never had first-aid training, you can still be of service, just by holding the victim's hand and calming them down (assuming his or her hands aren't mangled or something). Carry a handkerchief with you always, and you can provide a nice bandage. Let them keep the hankie. Carry a cell phone, too.

158 Challenge an opponent to a competitive two-player video game.

☠ ☠

Going head-to-head, you have to win by sheer skill—usually with some bravado and tenacity thrown in. This can ruin relationships.

159 Challenge a fourteen-year-old to a video game competition.

☠☠

They've got the hand-eye coordination, the experience, the know-how, and the will to sit still for sixteen hours straight, playing the same game over and over (mostly because they're not getting laid, and need to channel that energy). You think you can take one in a fair fight? Doubtful, friend—doubtful.

160 Testify in court.

☠☠☠

Yeah, they really want to hear from you, and they really want to hear the truth. You can best serve the commonweal by acting as a witness to a crime: Even though you could probably have more fun spending your time in other ways, and you're opening yourself up to all sorts of risk, this is really the right thing to do, if asked. Give it your best shot.

#160

161 Testify in court against someone dangerous and vindictive.

☠☠☠☠–☠☠☠☠☠, depending on circumstances

If you face personal danger in exchange for your testimony, with only the hope of the court's discretion in locking away the object of your declarations, then you are indeed living up to your responsibilities as a citizen.

162 Attend a meeting of a local government body.

☠☠

Although it is eminently tempting, do not bring a pillow. Sure, few things are more boring than sitting through a discussion among your city council regarding what kind of wildflowers to plant along the newly paved road, but snoring is frowned on.

IT'S SOMETIMES GOOD TO KNOW WHAT YOUR ELECTED OFFICIALS ARE UP TO. KEEP 'EM AS HONEST AS YOU CAN.

163 Reproduce.

☠☠☠☠☠

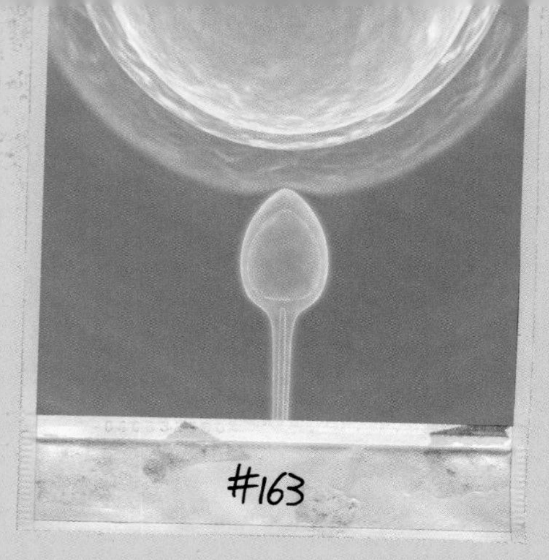

Okay, it doesn't seem like a big accomplishment, since pretty much everyone in history has done it (which is what gives us history, of course), but when you take into account everything that could go wrong, the cost involved, the duration of the obligation, the lost sleep, and other trade-offs, this is a grueling, ugly, expensive, hazard-prone activity. If done properly.

164 Reproduce more than once.

☠☠☠☠☠

Repeat for effect.

165 Be present during human reproduction.

☠☠☠

I'm referring to the really gross part, the part involving the placenta and such. Not the other gross part, conception.

Throw off whatever yoke your parents saddled you with.

☠ ☠ ☠ ☠

Maybe it was a religion, maybe it was a cultural notion, could be a language, or even a ridiculous behavior pattern left over from the country of their ancestors. This can be one of the most difficult to overcome; we're all little sponge-brains when we're young, absorbing whatever idiocy is presented to us.

IT CAN TAKE YEARS OF PERSONAL OBSERVATION AND EXPERIENCE BEFORE WE ARE ABLE TO REFUTE OUR PARENTS' EARLY NONSENSICAL RAVINGS.

Plot, then exact, your revenge.

☠ – ☠ ☠ ☠ ☠ ☠, depending on circumstances

Somebody's done something to you—oh yes, they have. Something that merits an act of vengeance. So be methodical, and choose a means that is appropriate and of like degree. And, hey—contrary to popular opinion, it is not a dish best served cold; by the time it's cold, revenge is all congealed and unsatisfying. Go for the hot stuff, baby.

Observe/participate in an autopsy.

☠☠

There's something that's just, well, creepy about cutting into a human corpse. Most of us try to avoid spending time around dead bodies, as it's just something that is cause for squeamishness. Take a gander at the procedure some time, and see if it's as gross as you've imagined.

Start a rumor.

☠ – ☠☠, depending on conditions

Anyone can retransmit some misinformation; that's no accomplishment. Starting your very own juicy bit of social infection, well, that's a different story. Try to come up with the kind of meme that will really spread, something that transcends your social circle and subculture, something that will travel the globe. It's much easier today, what with e-mail and the Internet and such, so for a really impressive Thing, try to foment your attack on the public record using only word-of-mouth.

BE SURE YOU'RE BEING ORIGINAL: CHECK *WWW.SNOPES.COM* TO ENSURE THAT YOU'RE NOT JUST REPLICATING SOMEONE ELSE'S RUMOR.

170 Introduce yourself to a stranger.

☠ ☠

It is quite likely, according to all the knowledge we've gathered from archeological and anthropological study, that the human creature's default decision regarding any other human not known to them is to assume a hostile, fatal stance, with ambush overtures when possible. This is probably because human beings are the most deadly, evil, vicious animals ever devised by nature, and have a proven record of conducting themselves accordingly. So our hereditary hesitancy against gregariousness, supported by our cultural mores toward insulation, are simply another set of defense mechanisms. Don't listen to them—the more people you know, the better your life will be. Trust me on this.

171 Introduce yourself to a stranger while traveling.

☠ ☠

Someone's sitting right next to you, crammed into that space you'll share for the duration of the trip. It's someone you've never met before, but you'll be amazed how much you have in common. Try to read the signals, though—if the other person doesn't feel like being sociable, shut up and keep to yourself.

172 Meet one of your heroes.

☠☠

You want them to be perfect, just the way you envisioned them: paragons of sense and objectivity, brimming with wisdom, monumentally talented. Most of the time, they're just people. For some reason, that becomes a real kick in the teeth. Oh, like the rest of us are any better, right?

173 Meet one of your fans.

☠☠☠

It is absolutely impossible to live up to the expectations of those who adulate you, especially if the reason you're being adored is something you've created, instead of something you are. The reverent expect you to be perfect, and kind, and wonderful, when you're really just that same jackass you ever were.

#173

174 Pick a fight with a neighbor.

☠☠☠☠

Keep in mind that they're going to be near you for a while.

175 Enter a contest judged solely (or mainly) on physical attractiveness.

☠☠

There are some people who are into extreme forms of sexual fetishism with a large dose of humiliation as the theme; even the kinkiest, wildest, most perverted yokel in the world has no clue what true degradation feels like, and that experience is not born in torture chambers or prisons or anything like that. The most severe form of humiliation is the beauty contest, where voluntary entrants are judged on the basis of their appearance, by other fallible humans.

176 Hitchhike.

☠ ☠

Free transport, right? Your car broke down, you don't have bus fare, you missed the train. So you stick out a thumb and try to bum a ride. In certain parts of the country, this practice is not only legal, but semiformalized: where carpooling is encouraged by government mandate, little cluster spots for "slugs" are arranged.

HITCHHIKING IS THE MOST UN-AMERICAN THING EVER DEVISED. A REAL AMERICAN DRIVES A CAR, RIDES A HORSE, OR WALKS. EXCEPT FOR BRUCE BANNER.

177 Pick up a hitchhiker.

☠ ☠

You can forget everything you might have assumed about hitchhiking, having done your research by watching porno movies. Likewise, you can ditch all the crazed notions set forth in those made-for-TV movies, too. Odds are, you are going to pick up neither a gorgeous sexual dynamo nor a psychopathic serial killer. What you are most likely to get is some scruffy, underwashed European backpacker or common vagrant. Yuck.

178 Shave/wax/remove hair from a part of your body where you don't normally shave/wax/remove hair from your body.

☠

Your skull, perhaps. Eyebrows. Other places. You'll get some looks the first few days, but those won't bother you nearly as much as the stubble when the stuff starts to regrow.

179 Shave using a straight razor.

☠ ☠

There's no need, with modern technology, to expose yourself to the dangers of this activity. And yet, there's a certain cachet in utilizing archaic devices for everyday purposes—it makes a hell of an affectation. Plus, you get a really close shave.

180 Radically change your appearance.

☠

Whatever anyone says otherwise, looks are extremely important; we judge each other by outward appearance, both upon first and subsequent meetings. Once you are known as having a certain "look" to you, everyone who knows you expects you to look that way in perpetuity. If you do something fairly minor, such as removing some of the hair from your face or skull, adopting a new mode of dress, or even just using some type of normal cosmetic in a way atypical for you, those who know you will treat you differently (for a while, anyway). It's an interesting phenomenon, and a cool experience.

181 Radically change your appearance with surgery.

☠ - ☠☠☠☠☠,
depending on severity

Don't like the way you look? Well, we have the capability to change that. There is virtually no limit to the modifications currently available to the human form. Try something different, interesting: Get an elephantine trunk placed on your face, or a peacock's feathers at the base of your spine. I mean, if you're going to do it, do it whole hog.

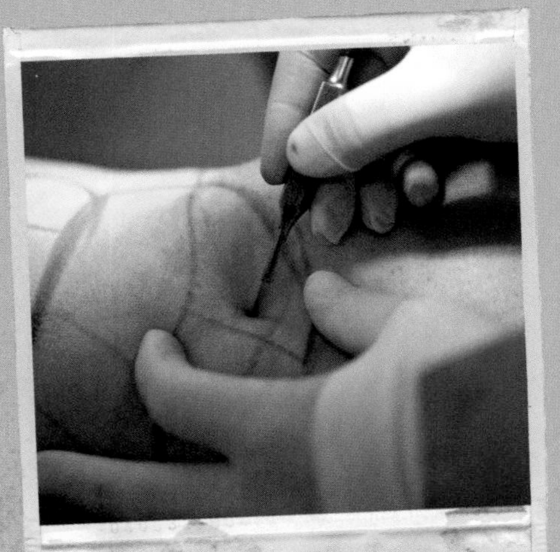

#181

Visit a hospice/nursing home/veterans' hospital on any holiday.

☠☠☠☠

This is about challenging yourself: Go ahead, go and have a look. See what it looks like to be alone, to be warehoused at the tail end of life. This is an optimum moment to decide how you're going to plan for your later days: Accumulate wealth so that you can pay for people to surround you with comfort and praise; breed manically, in the hopes one or more of your spawn will take care of that aspect of your endgame; ensure that you have a game plan, based on either age or condition, for when you will peacefully and responsibly check yourself out of Chez Life; or possibly some other option I haven't considered.

THIS IS NOT A DARE ABOUT FEELING GOOD. AND IT'S DAMN SURE NOT A DARE ABOUT MAKING OTHERS FEEL GOOD.

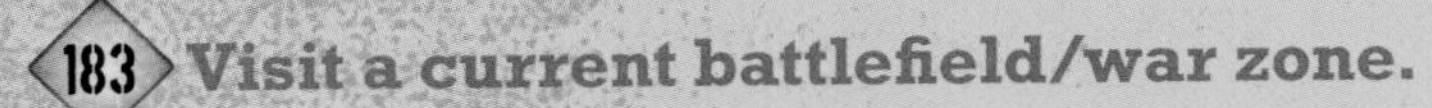

183 Visit a current battlefield/war zone.

☠☠☠☠☠

Think this one through first. Because you'd be going to a place where people are actually trying to kill other people. On purpose. This sounds like a really bad idea. Luckily, at any given time, there happen to be twenty-nine or so available on the planet, so you don't need to make reservations.

184 Spend eight hours straight holding a cardboard sign at a busy intersection.

☠☠

You will be amazed at a particular phenomenon, which eludes all psychological examination. Some people—total strangers!—will stop and give you money.

YOUR SIGN CAN READ ANYTHING YOU WANT: "HONK IF YOU LIKE MY BUTT," "WILL WORK FOR SPAM," OR "JESUS SAVES"—YOU GET THE IDEA.

185 While free from any infestation of your own offspring, baby-sit someone else's.

☠☠☠

You will never find a more demanding, stressful, infuriating activity. Try it for a minimum of six hours to get the full effect. This is quite possibly the best form of birth control ever devised—try it on your partner whenever he or she gets the bug to get some wee-beasties of your own.

186 Create a pilot for a reality-TV show.

☠☠☠

So, you think your life is interesting? Is it interesting enough that other people would want to watch it? Is it interesting enough that somebody will pay you to let other people watch it? Every now and then, various media outlets offer a chance to do this.

187 Engage in a game of mumblety-peg.

You throw or drop a knife and try to make it stick, blade-first, into the ground. Your opponents must mimic your technique. Groovy. And a cute way to perforate your foot.

188 Act as a mediator for opposing parties.

Sure, everyone's just talking. And you don't even have a dog in the fight. For some reason, if you have any judgment skills whatsoever, it will probably become rapidly apparent to you that one side, if not both, is full of poo-poo/ka-ka. Try to stay evenhanded.

189 Cultivate a distaste for something everyone else seems to like.

Say, children, or puppies. But, c'mon, really—who are you fooling? What kind of sick bastard hates puppies?

190 Never get married, even though you have a significant other.

☠☠☠☠

Our society hates this. Everyone really wants you to be married—mainly because they are married and can't stand the notion of anyone else escaping the curse. Of course, in actuality, there's very little reason to do so, but many reasons not to. Financially, marriage is a tax burden, and a method of losing everything in one fell swoop (the two of you are twined, inseparably). Legally, you're both one person, which hinders your combined ability to accomplish certain things; if you stay single, you can both purchase your own property and get much better rates than if you were linked.

LIVING HAPPILY IN SIN FOR YEARS ON END IS THE BEST REVENGE.

191 Live with a lover.

☠☠☠

There's been a taboo about this in our culture for a considerable amount of time. You get to see if your lover is one of those people who squeezes the toothpaste tube the wrong way. Yes, much of the romance might leave the relationship—but you can find out if there's anything else of substance to keep you together.

192 Go without toilet paper for a week.

☠ ☠ ☠

Of all the wonders and comforts afforded us, from making fire to genetic manipulation, it might suck most to not have toilet paper. Toilet paper is magic.

193 Survive a stabbing.

☠ ☠ ☠ ☠

The human body is a big mushy bag full of liquids. If you puncture that bag, or any of the many bags tucked inside (like so many gooey Russian nesting dolls), bad, bad things will happen, the very least of which is having the slop drip out; the liquids can merge and mix, which is more than awful. Do your best to avoid any punctures.

Survive a gunshot wound.

☠☠☠☠☠

Guns are designed to chuck a piece of metal at a target, at speeds high enough to punch a hole in it. We know this. It is also important to understand that a human body does not withstand holes created by high-velocity metal very well; in addition to the damage the piece of metal makes in its own right, there are additional concerns, such as hydrostatic shock, sepsis, bone shrapnel, etc. Understanding this is important because you never want to endure it. If you do, and survive, you are quite lucky.

Survive a snakebite.

☠☠☠–☠☠☠☠☠, depending on conditions

Snake venom is pretty deadly. But poisonous snakes only get one or two good shots in, and those fanged attacks make nice, neat little holes, and antivenin for snakes common to any geographical area is usually available in medical centers nearby. Snakes without fangs, such as constrictors, have rings of sharp cartilage "teeth," designed to penetrate the skin and flesh of their prey, and snag there. There are also plenty of exotic and dangerous bacteria inside a nonvenomous snake's mouth.

MANY NONVENOMOUS SNAKES HAVE SALIVA THAT CONTAINS ANTICOAGULANTS, CREATING WOUNDS THAT BLEED PROFUSELY FOR A LONG TIME.

196 Live among a culture wholly distinct from yours, with a primitive people.

☠☠☠☠☠

The greatest of anthropological challenges, this is the baseline from which all other societal norms are measured. To think that you could stay among these people and not impact their notions of their own society is ludicrous; trying to do so, in an effort to keep their own culture "intact," is absurd, and just as monstrous as anything they might do out of habit or tradition.

197 Attend a Greek festivity.

☠☠

This will involve some of the best-tasting food on the planet, plenty of alcoholic beverages, some dark, gorgeous people, and—no kidding—a lot of broken flatware.

I'M NOT SURE QUITE HOW SMASHING PLATES BECAME AN ELEMENT OF CELEBRATORY ACTIVITIES, BUT IT'S ENJOYABLE ENOUGH TO REALLY MAKE AN EVENT SPECIAL.

FINANCIAL THINGS They say money can't buy you happiness. They are chumps. While happiness might not be available on the store shelf right next to the deodorant and masking tape, it is one heck of a lot easier to be happier with money than without it. And, as adult behavior in a civilized world demands a constant exercise of informed decision-making, you continually are putting your money—and happiness—at risk. Do proper cost-benefit analysis. Stay rational and objective. Hire a professional. You might still lose everything, anyway.

198 Apply for a job for which you have no inherent or learned skills, talent, or disposition.

☠☠

Hey—the worst they can say is "no."

199 Quit your job.

☠☠

Walking away from a continual source of sustenance and support is an incredibly difficult thing to do. Even in the best circumstances, there is always a feeling of panic and plenty of room for second-guessing. This is extremely worthwhile.

200 Quit your job in dramatic fashion.

☠☠☠

Tell your boss to do something anatomically impossible. Joyously shout your renouncement of your soon-to-be-former employer in full view and hearing of your colleagues. Burn your bridges, and make sure you torched 'em good.

WALK AWAY FROM YOUR JOB KNOWING THAT DOOR IS CLOSED FOREVER.

201 Quit your job without having another lined up.

☠☠☠☠

Sometimes, well, sometimes you really can't stand what you're doing on a day-to-day basis. You loathe waking each morning, because it means another stretch of doing something you find utterly reprehensible. Nothing is worth that—no amount of money can make up for the misery you're going through. Just pull the plug and walk away; you probably won't starve, and you can always find something else.

202 Quit your job without having another lined up, move to another country without a visa, and start from scratch.

☠☠☠☠☠

Nearly every country on the planet has its own rules for allowing foreigners to live there and work. These rules are pretty strict and difficult to avoid. If you didn't know it before, you've read it here, so now you know. Not to say that it can't be done. . . .

203 Fire someone.

☠☠☠☠

You'd be amazed how many sundry difficulties this brings into play, even when the action is totally appropriate. It can often cause almost as many problems as it solves. A crying shame.

#203

204 Gamble in Vegas.

☠ ☠ ☠

This is the big-time. The no-kidding, how-you-do-it, down-and-dirty way to wager. You've got a system? Great—see all those big buildings with all the flashing lights and fancy gewgaws? Those were built by money taken from people with "systems." But go ahead and try, anyway. Hey, it's only money, right?

205 Gamble in an illegal setting.

☠ ☠ ☠ ☠ ☠

This is one of those "victimless" crimes . . . assuming you don't do the wrong thing, or end up in the wrong place at the wrong time—then you could, quite feasibly, become the victim. Of course, just by going to an illegal gambling venue, you're pretty much ensuring that you're in the wrong place.

#205

206 Play at least one game against a pool shark.

☠☠

We're talking billiards here: eight-ball, nine-ball, etc. Not an actual shark in a swimming pool, of course. Play to lose, and see what your opponent does. . . . Pool sharks are conditioned to let the "mark" (you) win the first couple of games, so as to get you to bet more money. This can be fun.

207 Start your own business.

☠☠☠☠

America is the land of opportunity. It was started with the notion that everyone should be allowed to make as much money as possible, and the best way to do that is to start your own business. But—starting your own business can also be a pretty sure-fire way to lose all your money.

ACCORDING TO THE SMALL BUSINESS ADMINISTRATION, ONE OUT OF EVERY THREE NEW BUSINESSES FAIL IN THE FIRST FOUR YEARS OF EXISTENCE.

208 Go into business with a family member.

☠ ☠ ☠ ☠

There are those who say stuff like, "Blood is thicker than water." Okay, but is it thicker than your bankbook?

WORKING WITH RELATIVES IS A GOOD WAY TO GET OUT OF HAVING TO DEAL WITH YOUR FAMILY EVER AGAIN.

209 Tell the IRS that they're wrong.

☠ ☠ ☠ ☠

They just love to hear that. They have entire departments full of people dedicated to helping you resolve your problem. Sadly, all those departments and all those people are given the assistance of lots and lots of computers, all specifically designed to follow processes that will make it nearly impossible for them to change any incorrect information in your file, while faithfully preserving all the incorrect information about you until the end of time.

210 Buy a house.

☠☠☠

This is an awkward, complicated, nerve-wracking process impeded by the best efforts of an entire industry created to take whatever money it can from you. The real estate agents, the lawyers, the appraisers, the mortgage brokers, the quasi-government "loan-guarantee" institutions—they all want to take a taste of your American pie. And we let them, only because the vast amounts of paperwork we have to deal with when purchasing a house totally boggles our minds, giving them the time to swoop in and carve out a piece, like vultures.

211 Buy a house in a foreign country.

☠☠☠☠

This can be an interesting experiment: Take out a stopwatch at the beginning of the process and try to find out exactly how long it takes you to get screwed.

212 Sell a house.

☠☠☠☠

This is almost always a bad idea. You'll never get as much as you thought you were going to, even if it sells at a higher price than you asked, after all the taxes and fees and commissions and whatnot. Better to rent it out.

213 Rent out a house.

☠☠☠

Oh, you wanted an exercise in pain? Here you go. Try renting to what starts as a small family, which incrementally grows into a large, extended "family" over a short period of time—a family comprised of the sort of people who threaten the neighbors with machetes, and who claim that they've already paid their rent, even when they clearly haven't.

#213

214 Buy a car.

For some reason, this has become a grueling process for everyone involved—including the customer. This is an utterly ridiculous situation: You want to buy something, the vendor wants to sell it to you, but there's an annoying little dance we must perform before completing the transaction.

215 Buy a used car.

Common understanding suggests that purchasing a used vehicle is a means of acquiring someone else's problems. Yet, on the flip side, common understanding also declares that a new vehicle loses up to one-third of its value when driven off the dealer's lot. Both, sadly, are true.

216 Work in a freelance capacity, for more than a month.

☠☠☠

Without a steady paycheck, it's hard to plan ahead. And in the world of freelance, even with "guaranteed" contracts worked out in advance, you are still at the discretion of the customer, who may or may not pay you in due time. The longer you do this, the easier it becomes, as you will have a nice backlog of receivables waiting for you.

217 Attend a live auction.

☠☠

The operative word of this Thing is live—not virtual, not online, but LIVE. You actually have to pick your butt up and go somewhere to do this. Once there, bid on something. Do not drink—buzzed bidding is directly responsible for over half the inane auction purchases in this country alone.

THE BIG DARE OF GOING TO A LIVE AUCTION IS TO LEAVE WITHOUT HAVING PURCHASED ANYTHING.

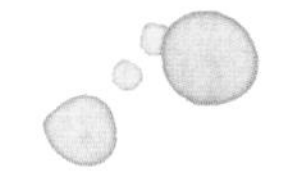

218 File a lawsuit.

☠☠

It's the modern American hobby. There are an unlimited amount of reasons you can sue someone. Try to keep in mind that the only people who win lawsuits are the lawyers.

219 Negotiate a contract.

☠☠

Contrary to popular belief, everything is negotiable. The terms of your mortgage, your car financing, even an oath of office are all contracts you are free to enter (or not enter); you can change the terms of those contracts as you see fit. Hey, the worst the other party can do is say "no." You'd be surprised how much folks are willing to concede, if you just ask for it.

220 While negotiating a contract, make a ludicrously insane request.

☠☠☠

How will you know exactly how desperate the other party is, unless you test said party with a contractual condition that is totally outside the bounds of reason?

221 Try growing something for profit.

☠☠☠☠

Okay, Farmer Brown, take your best whack at it. You'll be glad to know that the entire resources of the Department of Agriculture are at your disposal, and you can get crop insurance, and that there are price supports and subsidies for just about everything grown in this country. Not many other business ventures give you a "do-over" if you screw up.

OF COURSE, FARMING IS ALSO ONE OF THE MOST DIFFICULT, GRUELING, ARCHAIC, DEMEANING WAYS TO RAISE REVENUE. MORE POWER TO YOU.

222 Barter.

☠

There are those snobs who suggest that bartering is an archaic, unsophisticated form of transaction, and that modern commerce is much more complex. They have it exactly backwards: The reason money is used today is that it makes transactions much simpler and, therefore, much less sophisticated. When all you have is a set of goods, and you want to exchange some of your goods for some of somebody else's, you are dealing with the true high art of the free market. You can also lose your shirt.

223 Haggle with a vendor at an open-air market.

☠

This should be performed in a foreign country for best effect, where both you and the other party have only cursory knowledge of each other's language, but you can often find similar circumstances in your own state or city. These people are the world's most ideal capitalist entrepreneurs. Check for a price—there probably isn't one. Let them throw out an offer. Ask if that's the best offer. Make a counteroffer. Repeat for effect. Never, ever fall in love with the object you wish to purchase—if you do, you have killed your ability for true negotiation.

224 Haggle at an American flea market.

☠ ☠

They might look like rejects from a casting call for actors with distinguishing hillbilly traits, but these are probably some of the sharpest businesspeople in the country. Not an inch, not a bit will they budge. Good for them.

#223

225 Conduct cold-call sales over the phone.

☠

Go ahead—bother people at home, or at their place of work. Ask them if they want something they obviously don't need. Pester them until they either hang up or buy whatever it is you're selling. At least they can't punch you over the phone.

226 Conduct cold-call sales door-to-door.

☠

If you're over the age of twelve, this is no longer adorable. In fact, it's just annoying. You are basically trespassing, and for sure pissing people off.

Homestead a vacant plot of land.

There are still places on this planet that you can own by simply going there and setting up house. Of course, they're out in the, well, I can't say they're in the middle of nowhere, because that implies that there's some border and shape to "nowhere," which is not the case—these pieces of land are nowhere.

Homestead in Alaska.

Not only do you have to choose a nowhere location, but you also have to pick a cold one. You have to be a resident of the state to apply.

Stake a mining claim.

Yes, it's bizarre, but staking your own claim is not some archaic form of acquiring mining rights, a relic from black-and-white movies about the Gold Rush: You, too, can be a miner, with your own plot of land, just by finding some empty parcel and staking it out. Check your local laws, buy a pickax, and go get rich!

"STAKING" A CLAIM MEANS TO LITERALLY PUT DOWN STAKES AT THE CORNERS OF YOUR PLOT, DESIGNATING ITS LOCATION AND PERIMETER.

230 Squat on a piece of property.

☠ ☠ ☠

Possibly the lowest form of legalized theft, you can rip off some real estate by just sitting on it for a given length of time. Better hope the rightful owners don't catch you before the time limit expires. Check all local laws.

Trespass.

☠ – ☠ ☠ ☠ ☠ ☠, depending on locale

If you're going to do this, make it grandiose—don't just cut through the neighbor's backyard. Make it a real daring event. Climb the fence of a junkyard protected by attack dogs; wander into a construction site. This is, yes, illegal.

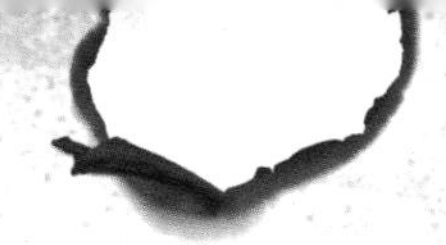

232 Invest in the stock market.

☠☠☠☠

Don't let anyone tell you differently: Buying and selling openly traded stocks is just like any other form of gambling—there is no guarantee you're going to make money, no matter how you do it. And the term *openly traded* can be a bit of a misnomer, too; often, you need to purchase the services of a broker or agent or arbiter of some sort, which cuts into your profits. There are plenty of stock markets to choose from, from the well-known New York Stock Exchange, to the Tokyo.

YOU MIGHT TRY THE CHICAGO STOCK EXCHANGE, WHICH IS A LOT LESS PRETENTIOUS THAN THE OTHERS.

233 Invest in fine wine.

☠☠☠☠

This is the kind of gamble in which you can take a bath; a metaphorical bath, to be sure, because actually, literally bathing in wine is just silly. If you're really going to do it, you've got to invest in one of those wine cellar things, either a real one in your house or a portable, plug-in type.

234 Buy someone a living thing as a gift.

☠☠☠☠

This is one of the riskiest things you can do for someone you love, or even like. They may like it, or they may take offense; this is right up there with demeaning their skills as a lover or yanking bits of their body away from the rest of it without benefit of anesthesia. A pet is a commitment of both time and money, and a heady responsibility—it's a living creature, which will only remain living at the expense (of both time and funds) of the owner.

IMPOSING A LIVING CREATURE ON AN UNSUSPECTING PERSON CAN YIELD UNPREDICTABLE RESULTS.

235 Invest in fine art.

☠☠☠☠

Unless you know what you're doing, and you have excellent timing, this is strictly for those who have plenty of disposable cash.

236 Invest in commodities.

☠☠☠☠

Sounds fancy, don't it? Well, the word *commodities* is just a highfalutin way of saying "stuff." So, you're buying "stuff." Or, even worse, you're buying the opportunity to sell stuff at a certain price. You better hope your stuff remains valuable—at least as valuable as the price you paid. Otherwise, guess what?

237 Invest in foreign currency.

☠☠☠☠☠

Okay, get this: you're betting that the price of your money is going to be better (lower or higher, depending on your trade) than some other country's money. Now, how silly is that? Why not just try honest gambling?

238 Join a union.

☠ ☠ ☠

Give up your individual right to create your own contract, reduce your worth to that of your lowest colleague, and start paying dues.

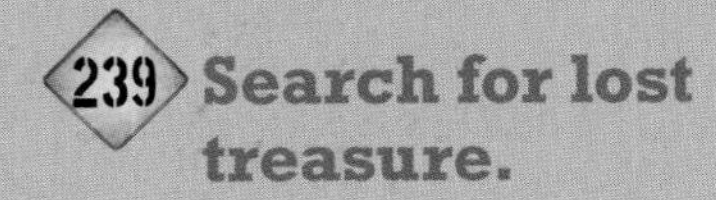

239 Search for lost treasure.

☠ ☠ ☠ ☠

There's supposedly a whole bunch of it out there. All you have to do is find it. Of course, if it were easy, someone would have already picked it up. Which would mean it wouldn't be "lost" anymore. There's a reason it's stayed lost. You can go broke trying to get rich.

POLITICAL THINGS In the United States, we have a participatory government, which means that old people vote religiously, and a certain minority of goofballs, groomed from youth or with a megalomaniacal bent, run for all offices. But that shouldn't stop you—jump in!

Attend a public demonstration of some sort.

☠ ☠

Go to any demonstration, any public protest against anything—any cause, any activity, any person, any group. Walk around. See people yelling and waving signs. Look at all the other people voicing their opinions for their own causes (either allied with or opposed to the main demonstration). Watch how much goofier those tertiary groups become, as you move out toward the fringes. Strange bedfellows, indeed.

REMEMBER THE OLD SAYING, "POLITICS MAKES FOR STRANGE BEDFELLOWS."

Vote for a candidate who has no possible way of winning whatsoever.

☠ ☠

This is the American Way. Sure, anybody can pick a candidate who is probably going to win—what's the point of having democracy if you don't push the limits?

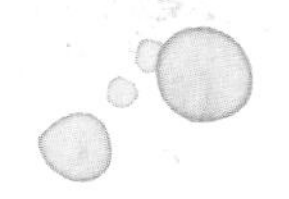

242 Start your own political party.

☠☠☠☠

There's a history of outstanding Americans who have decided that the mainstream groups just aren't meeting their needs, so they went out and started their own. Such as the founders of this country. Or, Mark Twain, who was a proud Mugwump. Use these icons as heroes, and go for it.

243 Join a political party that is not one of the "Big Two."

Maybe you don't really want to start your own political party; maybe that sounds like too much work. No big deal—there are plenty from which to choose.

DID YOU KNOW THE AMERICAN COMMUNIST PARTY IS STILL AROUND? THEY EVEN HAVE A WEB SITE: *WWW.CPUSA.ORG.*

244 Run for public office.

☠☠☠

You don't have to shoot for the brass ring or anything—hold off announcing your candidacy for the presidency. Start small, like running for chief of the local water district or something. You'd be surprised how many votes you get just for being on the ballot.

245 Emigrate from your homeland.

☠☠☠☠

For whatever reason, you don't like the place where you were born. So now you've got to pick somewhere else to live. Not the simplest of procedures, but getting easier as technology evolves.

246 Ask another nation for asylum.

☠☠☠☠

Not only don't you want to live in the place you're from, but they would really like to hurt you if you went back. This is an advanced form of guilt-tripping someone into a gesture of pity, and a pretty important one, at that.

#246

ARTISTIC THINGS Creative accomplishment is pretty much a human endeavor; there are the odd apes or elephants who do some painting, and a few chimps with acting careers, and the vast majority of Web site design is performed by lemurs, but that's about all the animal kingdom contributes to the world's artistic collection. So be a proud member of your species: Do something creative. It's your birthright.

247 Write a book.

☠ ☠

Stringing a bunch of words together is not nearly as difficult as writers would have you think. Stringing a bunch of words together that are worth reading, on the other hand, takes some diligence and patience.

248 Participate in an open-mic night at a comedy club and bomb.

☠ ☠ ☠

It's a miserable, excruciating experience. There is nothing quite like it.

VETERAN COMEDIANS DREAD BOMBING EVERY MOMENT OF THEIR LIVES (INCLUDING WHEN THEY SLEEP, DURING WHICH TIME THEY DREAM ABOUT IT).

249 Participate in improvisational comedy.

☠☠☠☠

Much more difficult than performing scripted comedy (which, in itself, is a bitter challenge).

250 Audition for a play.

☠☠

You don't have to actually get the part, but trying out is an excellent exercise in humility and bravado. Go for it. It can be a lot of fun. No kidding.

251 Act in a play in public.

☠☠☠

Pretending to be somebody else can be very rewarding—and pretending to be somebody else who is really unlike you can be really difficult and humiliating. Doing it in front of strangers is all of that.

252 Learn an exotic dance.

☠ ☠ ☠

There are myriad forms of rhythmic, physical forms of self-expression; some are kooky, some are painful and challenging, and some are downright sexy. Pick something you can use to show off. Tango, rumba, hip-hop, waltz, ballet, flamenco, polka, tap, even the Charleston.

253 Dance in public.

☠ ☠ ☠

You'll never look as goofy as you think you look. Really. Just jumping up and kicking out the jams is extremely liberating, and even those who deride you will be totally jealous of your ability to let it all hang out.

254 Sing in public.

Yes, you really do sound silly. Unlike dancing, you can't possibly sound as good as you think you do. Still, your audience will be forgiving, because this takes a great deal of courage.

IF YOU WANT A BRUTALLY CRITICAL AUDIENCE FOR YOUR SINGING, CHARGE ADMISSION.

255 Cut a record.

You think your music is so good that other people will pay to have their very own copy of it. Granted "cutting" a "record" is kind of an archaic way of denoting this activity, but it's got the cachet of historical notoriety. Knock yourself out.

256 Paint a full-sized painting on canvas.

☠

You might reveal that nascent talent, that sliver of disguised promise, that makes you the next Rembrandt.

THE WORST POSSIBLE RESULT FROM YOUR PAINTING IS THAT YOU WILL DESTROY SOME CANVAS WITH AN ARTWORK SO BAD THAT YOUR PETS WILL GO INTO SEIZURES FROM LOOKING AT IT.

257 Try to sell your art.

☠ ☠ ☠

Just because your efforts may have cost you a great deal of money and time, and might have great sentimental value for you, this does not mean that anyone else will place any value whatsoever on your work.

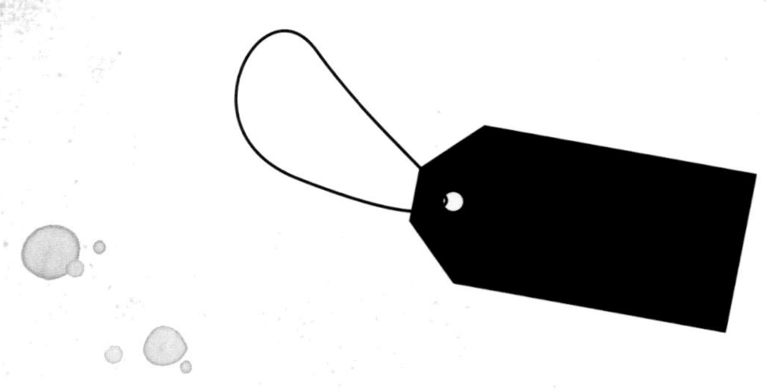

258 Participate in a radio broadcast.

☠☠

Let people hear what you have to say. . . . Odds are, it's pretty boring, but no less boring than whatever else happens to be on the radio. If you really want to be daring, do a live broadcast. Be sure to get a tape of the program, because, yes, you really do sound like that.

259 Try to win a contest sponsored by a radio station.

☠☠

I've done this, mostly when I was a kid. I was successful a couple times, too. Most recently, while writing this silly book, I stumped movie guy Jeff Howard with a question about the film *Miller's Crossing*. I rock.

260 Try out for a television game show.

☠ ☠ ☠

You can't possibly be as stupid as most of the people who participate in those things. Unfortunately, you probably have too much personality.

261 Participate in a television broadcast.

☠ ☠ ☠

Now you can know what you really look and sound like. There's plenty of junk on television already, so no matter how lame your appearance turns out to be, you will definitely be better than most of the stuff on prime time.

TRY NOT TO THINK ABOUT ALL THOSE PEOPLE STARING AT YOU; SOME WILL HAVE SICK FANTASIES ABOUT YOU NO MATTER HOW UNATTRACTIVE YOU ARE.

262 Participate in a live television broadcast.

☠ ☠ ☠ ☠

You have no idea what stupid thing you might say or do—which increases your nervousness, which increases the chances of you saying or doing something stupid, ad infinitum.

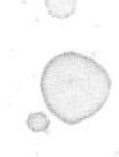

263 Get pierced through your nipple.

☠

When I was growing up, one of the most abusive means of torturing your siblings and contemporaries was the "titty twister," whereby the antagonist grabbed the nipple of the victim, yanked, and put sufficient torque on the anatomy to cause incapacitating pain. Nowadays, instead of a demeaning attack on the unwary among your age demographic, it is a fashion trend.

264 Get pierced through your genitalia.

☠

You're—going to—do what? To what? No, really—really? Uhhh . . . okay. I guess. I mean—wait—really? No foolin'? Um . . . how come? I mean . . . no—wait. Really?

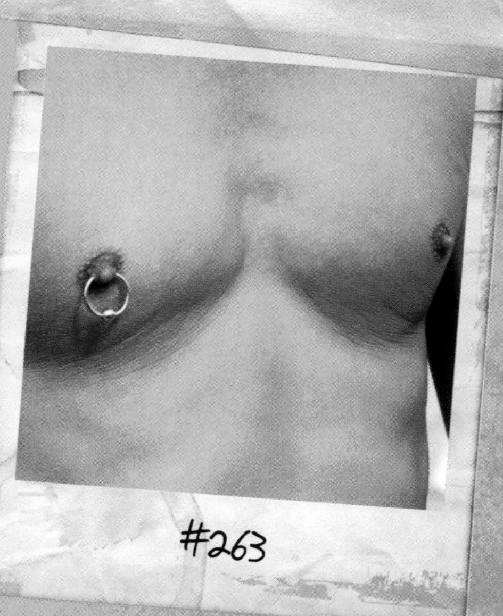

265 Get a tattoo.

☠

What possible thing could you put on your body that you'd want to see thirty years from now? No—stop and think about it for a second. Remember what you looked like/thought/said ten years ago? Was that person smart or talented or wonderful in any way? What makes you think that the person ten years from now is going to feel any different about you? But hey, maybe you'll receive the joy of hepatitis.

266 Get a tattoo on your face.

☠ ☠ ☠

Unless it's part of your tribal ritual, or you belong to a Maori culture, it's going to be difficult to justify this amendment of your features. Plus, head wounds bleed a lot. But hey, maybe you can offer your face for marketing purposes—it's worked before.

267 Be an extra in a feature film.

They're always looking for people—all kinds of people. You don't necessarily have to be attractive or in shape.

BEING AN EXTRA MOSTLY INVOLVES A LOT OF STANDING AROUND, TAKING CONFLICTING DIRECTION FROM VARIOUS CREW MEMBERS, AND FIGHTING OODLES OF BOREDOM.

268 Make your own movie.

No—home movies of your cute family and pets and silly friends do not count. We're talking about a real movie, with a plot, characters, and conflict. The technology is now ubiquitous, so you have no real excuse not to give it a go. Remember coming out of the theater thinking, "Boy, that sucked"? Well, demonstrate how you can do it better.

269 Engage in a poetry slam competition.

☠ ☠

These people are not here to play. They are not adherents of the "roses are red" school of literature. They are extremely serious, and they have a strident point to get across. And they are pretty damned tough.

270 Attend an artistic display performed entirely by children.

☠ ☠ ☠ ☠

There are few things quite as grueling than a mass of untalented, youthful amateurs trying to engage in artistic expression.

271 Invent something.

☠ ☠ ☠

Be sure to get it patented (at the United States Patent and Trademark Office, of course: *www.uspto.gov*). If it's useful, hey, so much the better.

ALMOST EVERYTHING WORTH DOING HAS BEEN DONE ALREADY; JUST ABOUT EVERYONE THINKS THEY HAVE A GREAT IDEA, BUT VERY FEW REALLY DO.

272 Complete the crossword puzzle in the Sunday edition of the *New York Times*.

☠ ☠ ☠

Better linguists than you or I have tried and failed. This is the big one. Go for it. Set yourself a time limit, or face the possibility of going slightly mad.

273 Make your own clothing.

☠ – ☠ ☠, depending on circumstances

The means for accomplishing this are almost limitless: weaving, knitting, sewing, baking (if you really want to be daring). But creating the actual garments themselves is not the apex of the Thing—wearing them in public is.

#273

274 Demolish a structure.

☠ – ☠ ☠ ☠ ☠ ☠, depending on conditions

For some reason, destroying something is immensely enjoyable—more enjoyable, even, than creating something. Maybe it's because the former doesn't usually involve as much attention to detail and planning. Unless, of course, your method of choice for demolition is explosives to cause an implosion.

275 Photograph a wild animal in its natural habitat.

☠ – ☠ ☠ ☠ ☠ ☠, depending on circumstances

Don't just pick a bunny rabbit or squirrel or something—for daring, stalk and shoot a panther or bear or hippo (on film). If you want a real challenge, and have the guts, don't use a telephoto lens. You can forgo asking your subjects to yell "Cheese."

276 Learn to throw your voice.

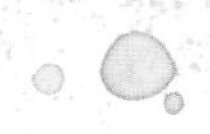

The much-maligned art of ventriloquism suffers from an image problem, probably as a result of all those evil, alcoholic, murderous ventriloquists. But just think of how many times being able to talk while you're drinking a glass of water will come in handy!

277 Learn some magic.

This doesn't have to be sawing your partner in half, or surviving a dunk tank while in a straitjacket or anything. You can learn a couple of little party tricks involving a deck of playing cards or coins or something.

IT'S ALWAYS NICE TO HAVE SOMETHING THAT WILL STARTLE OR AMAZE PEOPLE, AS LONG AS IT ISN'T TOO LAME.

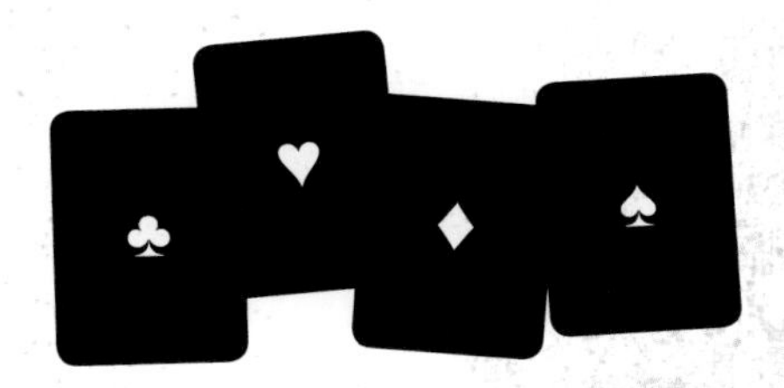

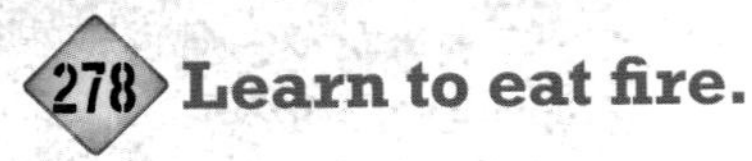

278 Learn to eat fire.

☠ ☠ ☠ ☠

Okay, so you're not actually eating fire. Instead, you use a combination of hand-eye coordination and the laws of physics. Anyone—even you—can eat fire. Of course, safety precautions are necessary (as with any use of fire), and a high pain threshold is desirable, as you will inevitably suffer burns to the lips, tongue, mouth, and throat.

FOR MORE INFO, VISIT THE WEB SITE OF THE NORTH AMERICAN FIRE ARTS ASSOCIATION: *WWW.NAFAA.ORG.*

279 Perform some taxidermy.

☠

This is all about stuffing an animal, and I don't mean with breading. Usually, this is a practice seen as creepy and asocial, reserved for the likes of Norman Bates and his alleged model, Ed Gein. Playing with dead animals can elicit this type of reaction, but so what? Who are you trying to impress? Get out your needle and thread and get to work!

280 Learn to play a musical instrument.

☠☠☠

It's not just about hand-eye coordination. It's not just about patience. It's not just about a natural inclination and talent for such things. It's about all of that, and more.

281 Write a news article.

☠☠☠

Sure, it can't be that hard—look at the people who do it. But actually doing it in a way that's somewhat accurate, getting all that information in the correct order, with a coherent narrative, and not inventing bits and pieces, well, that's pretty tough. Avoiding the response from your readers is not so easy, either.

282 Tag something with spray paint.

☠ ☠

Some call this vandalism; the authorities treat it as such—even when simultaneously taking your stolen tax dollars to finance ludicrous and crappy "public art." Go out and create your own public art, using the wonderful invention of paint in a pressurized can. Be creative—"Leonard Loves Micki" does not cut it. Oh, and it's illegal. So maybe you shouldn't.

283 Fell a tree with an ax.

☠ ☠

The tree is actually pretty good at sustaining a lot of damage—that's what it was bred to do. That's why there are still trees on this planet. It's going to take you a lot of chopping to pull this off, even for a skinny tree. You go, Paul Bunyan.

Fell a tree with a chainsaw.

☠☠

Okay, now we're talking. There's something about an engine you can hold in your hands, especially if it's powering a device with the destructive power offered by a chainsaw. Slicing wood with a chainsaw isn't like work—it's more like playtime for grownups. Even after you chop down the tree, then chop it up into manageable pieces, you're still going to want to do some more chopping. If you can swing it, take one of those old pieces of furniture you've been meaning to get rid of and . . . .

Slice up a piece of furniture with a chainsaw.

☠☠☠

There's really nothing like it. Talk about fun!

BE SURE TO WEAR GLOVES AND GOGGLES—NAILS AND SPRINGS AND OTHER STUFF ARE GOING TO COME FLYING OUT AT THE EQUIVALENT OF 275 MILES PER HOUR.

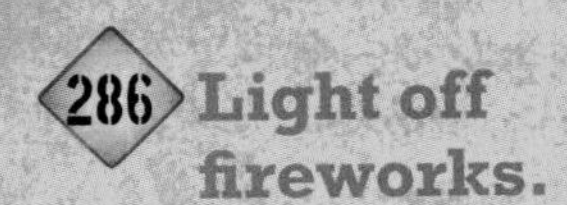

286 Light off fireworks.

☠

There are few things more archetypically American than causing explosions for no particular reason. Fireworks are just miniature explosives, manufactured in bulk, and quality-controlled for safety in home usage. Theoretically.

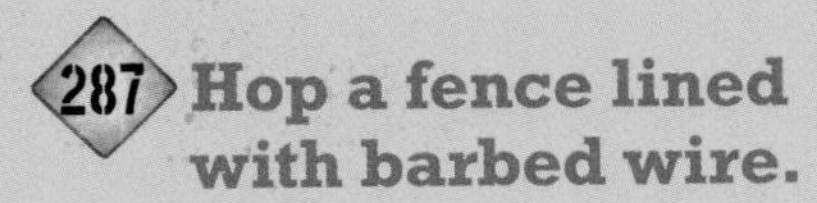

287 Hop a fence lined with barbed wire.

☠☠

Usually found on farms or wooded lots, this can be found in single- or multiple-strand configurations. The trick is to get over all the wire without getting hung up on barbs. Not too difficult for crafty humans; this is mainly to keep livestock in one place, and to keep them from getting ideas.

Learn to say "f--- you" in forty languages, one of which is spoken only in a small village in Africa.

Communication is about getting your point across. "F--- you" is about the most basic point imaginable.

"F--- YOU" IS ALSO INCREDIBLY FLEXIBLE—WITH THE PROPER INTONATION, INFLECTION, AND DELIVERY, IT CAN MEAN ALMOST ANYTHING.

Build your own Web site.

HTML. JavaScript. Perl. Whatever. You got something to say, in today's world, you say it online. And the really gutsy ones go and figure out how to do it for themselves, instead of letting someone else do the hosting and design.

Try to make money off a Web site.

Yeah, there was a time when they were giving money to anyone who could even spell "dot-com," but that time has long passed. And that's not necessarily a bad thing; you now have to have both a viable idea and a means to execute it before you can make money on the Internet. It's darned tough, even then.

291 Watch a foreign film.

☠

Foreigners do not think like us—that is what makes them foreign. Because of this, you will notice that foreign films often contain plot points, situations, and characters that make no sense to you, the viewer, whatsoever, but which the director assumed everyone would understand. This is probably why they're called "foreign films" instead of "foreign movies."

292 Make an igloo.

☠

You'd be surprised how easy it is. Well, how easy it is to build one that stays up for a little while. Use that good, wet, heavy packing snow. Sleep in it overnight.

Learn to be a sword-swallower.

☠☠☠☠☠

Yeah, take a long, sharp metal object and shove it down your throat. Sounds like a recipe for disaster, doesn't it? It does. And probably is. So be damned careful when going about the instructional process, and be sure not to leave a copy of this book around where someone might trip over it while trying to get you some medical attention.

Read someone else's unedited, unpublished book.

☠☠☠

Okay, for as few people there are that can string an idea out onto a page, using words instead of cartoons, there are even fewer who can do it at book length. While publishing may be an incestuous, backbiting, nasty, artificial little business, it at least serves the purpose of keeping most of the really crappy stuff away from an unsuspecting public.

SURE, SOME LOUSY BOOKS GET PUBLISHED—BUT YOU SHOULD SEE THE TRULY CRUMMY STUFF THAT NEVER MAKES IT OFF THE PUBLISHER'S DESK. . . .

295 Listen to another culture's music.

☠ ☠

Strangely, music is an art that is often particularly geared to a specific culture, at a specific time in history. Sure, there are certain tunes, melodies, and whatnot that can transcend time and populace, but those seem to be the exceptions, not the rule. Even more so than film, music can please a certain ear, and scrape against those not receptive to it.

296 Listen to an hour of music that was written over a hundred years ago.

☠

Classical music or opera accompanied by a Bugs Bunny cartoon does not count.

297 Listen to an hour of pop music written twenty years after you were born.

☠ ☠ ☠

This is not meant for you to enjoy. In fact, if done properly, it is specifically designed to annoy the living piss out of you.

IF NEW POP MUSIC DOESN'T ANNOY YOU, THEN YOUR GENERATION HAS ABSOLUTELY NO CREATIVITY, OR CULTURE TO CALL THEIR OWN. LOSERS.

298 Bathe a pet dog.

☠-☠☠☠☠, depending on circumstances

The difficulty of this really depends on the specific breed. Some dogs actually dig it. But, whether you've got a dog that is into bathing or not, you should prepare to get wet. Or maybe bit.

299 Bathe a wild animal, of any type.

☠☠☠☠

Not quite sure why you'd want to do this, but I imagine it would be really tricky. Because—the animal won't like it.

300 Go on tour.

☠☠☠

So your artistic gig is pleasing to enough people that you think you can hack it on the circuit? Well then, get out there! Stay in those hotels, eat that convention food, and do some hand exercises (for signing autographs, of course).

301 Shoe a horse.

☠☠☠☠

There's an art to smithing, which made it such a widespread trade back when horses were the preferred mode of transportation. Plus, horses need shoes. They are not exactly fond, however, of misplaced nails that strike the sensitive part of the hoof, and they are not at all forgiving of dumbassed humans.

#301

302 Build some furniture.

☠☠

Unlike other crafts, furniture is meant to be used. You're going to sit on it, or lie down on it, or put socks inside it, and it's going to have to be built well enough to provide whatever service you intended. So you're providing yourself with inherent risk. Cool.

303 Re-enact a scene from your favorite film.

☠☠☠

Try to refrain from comments about life imitating art, okay? It's sometimes a hoot to ape something you've always admired. Try to be cool about this, though—refrain if the movie you had in mind features zombies in prominent roles, or a scene in which the bank teller goes down on the pizza delivery guy.

304 Go to Tiffany's in Manhattan.

☠☠☠☠

Arrive with a tin ring and $50 (allowing for inflation). If you don't know the rest, you need to watch more movies.

305 Write your name in wet cement.

☠

Optimally, this will be wet cement that you own, so as not to infringe on someone else's wet cement.

LEAVING YOUR NAME IN CEMENT IS A LAME ATTEMPT AT IMMORTALITY BUT, FOR SOME OF US, IT'S THE BEST CHANCE WE'VE GOT. MAKE IT AS BIG AS POSSIBLE.

306 Create your own porn.

☠☠☠☠

Stills or full-motion video, whatever kind of stuff you want. Today it's easy, with digital cameras, InterCyberWeb. . . . Back in the day, you had to take the 110 to the Photomat, and trust the people inside.

307 Trust your significant other to hold onto the homemade porn.

☠☠☠☠☠

Sure, and right after that, give your lover the key to the safety deposit box, access to your firearms, and a medical power of attorney. Homemade porn is one of those things that is never destroyed, never goes away, is never lost—although it may be found by strangers—and has amazing transitional properties. They should make the space shuttle out of the stuff.

TRAVEL THINGS It's been suggested that the vast majority of individuals die within twelve miles of where they were born . . . without ever having left the immediate geophysical region during the interim. This, to me, is just sad: The planet is pretty big, and spending your entire life in one tiny corner of it seems like a lot of wasted opportunity. Get out of town—go explore, go see what's to see. Maybe you won't even like it elsewhere . . . but at least you'll die knowing you're happy with the place where you chose to die.

308 Travel to a foreign country.

Any country. Nothing will make you appreciate home quite as much as spending time elsewhere.

309 Travel to a foreign country where they don't speak English.

☠ ☠ ☠

That language barrier is a lot more daunting when you're faced with something more than just ordering a meal in an ethnic restaurant.

310 Travel to a foreign country where they don't speak English and they hate Americans.

☠ ☠ ☠

This isn't cute, it isn't fun, and it poses a real, constant danger. Be very, very careful.

FOR INCREASED SAFETY IN FOREIGN LANDS, PRETEND TO BE CANADIAN.

311 Travel to a foreign city under siege from terrorism.

☠ ☠ ☠ ☠

Terrorists are not bright people. Smart people don't grow up to choose "terrorizing others" as a job description, because there's not a big future in it. So foreign terrorists, by and large, think you are personally responsible for every ill our nation has perpetrated globally, and that we have wealthy families prepared to offer exorbitant ransoms for our safe return.

312 Backpack across a continent.

☠☠☠

Pick a small one, like Europe, where there are plenty of places to buy water and snacks. Europe also has hostels; hostel means "place where unkempt backpackers sleep and are robbed" in European.

313 Visit all seven continents.

☠☠☠☠

Antarctica is the really tricky one—you have to get permission, and/or have a pretty good reason to go there.

314 Go into the wilderness.

☠–☠☠☠☠☠, depending on locale

To those raised ensconced in concrete and steel, some trees, grass, and lots of stars can look awfully damned spooky. But it's really not all that bad; there are few things left that can kill you outright. In the American wilderness, anyway. Wilderness in another country like, say, Asia? You're dead.

Spend New Year's Eve in Times Square.

There are actually very few places where the word *throngs* is accurate and applicable in literature. It's a word often abused, as a way of saying "crowds" without sounding so pedestrian. Well, on New Year's Eve, in Times Square, you can safely use that word without fear of misusing it.

Spend New Year's Eve on the Vegas Strip.

Vegas is usually pretty crowded on any given day. On New Year's Eve, goofballs from all over the planet find it somehow pleasurable to congregate on the street outside the larger casinos and wander around drinking.

Spend Fat Tuesday in New Orleans.

Again, there seems to be some mystique in clustering with likeminded bumblef---s whom you don't know, for the express purpose of imbibing alcohol and walking up and down the street.

318 Visit Rio for Carnival.

☠☠☠

Carnival is not just about walking around and drinking; it's about walking around, drinking, dancing, and sex. Which seems a lot more interesting.

319 Spend spring break wherever the kids happen to be spending it this year.

☠☠

There have been many "hot" places for the traditional spring break gatherings over the years: Daytona, Fort Lauderdale, Lake Havasu, South Padre, Cancun, Scranton. . . . All the North American hotspots have been tapped at one time or another (and still are today).

IF YOU LIKE BEING AROUND A BUNCH OF IMMATURE DRUNKS, ALL OF WHOM ARE BENT ON PROPERTY DAMAGE AND NOISE, THEN SPRING BREAK IS THE PLACE FOR YOU!

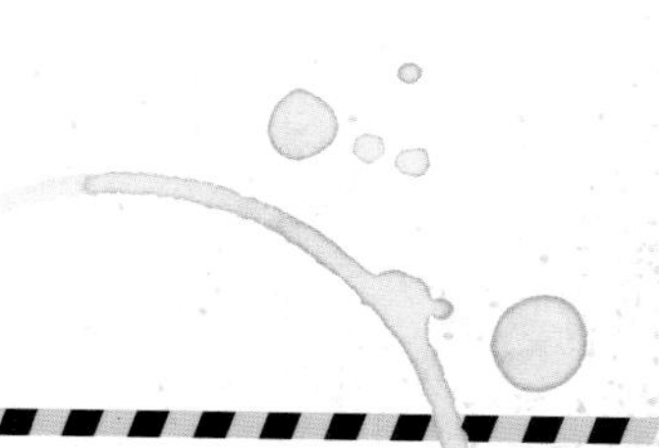

Go on safari in the African veldt.

There's some big, dangerous critters in that place. Really big, and really dangerous. Of course, the most dangerous African critters aren't big at all—it's the microscopic nasties that are so deadly. They got stuff that hasn't even been discovered yet, because whoever gets it just dies right there, so the sickness is never diagnosed. Be sure to get your shots first—as if that will help.

Go into the Australian bush.

It's big. So big, there's parts of it that have never been seen, up close and personal, by anything other than a dingo or bird. Sure—Qantas flies over, and it's been mapped very well . . . but it's still fairly empty. Take a good deal of water and a GPS.

322 Visit the Grand Canyon.

Yes, it's just a big hole in the ground. Which is like saying an orgasm is just an itch being scratched. Better writers than I have described it—so I won't even try. Just go and do it, dammit.

323 See the northern or southern lights (aurora borealis or australis).

You have go way up (or down) into some dreary polar latitudes to catch a glimpse of this phenomenon.

SOMETIMES, NOT TOO OFTEN, CONDITIONS WILL BE JUST RIGHT FOR YOU TO SEE THESE LIGHTS FROM ALMOST ANYWHERE IN THE NORTHERN HEMISPHERE.

324 See the Southern Cross.

Not nearly as amazing as the northern/southern lights. It's just some stars in the sky, and you can pretty much see stars from wherever you are. But these stars are only visible from the Southern Hemisphere, so it's a good excuse to get down to the Southern Hemisphere. Nice.

Cross an international border illegally.

☠ ☠ ☠ ☠

There are really very few places in the world where the demarcation between one nation and another is clearly defined by any tangible symbol. Most borders are literally only lines on a map. So walk, drive, swim, or fly across one or two. It shouldn't be too difficult.

I REMIND YOU: SNEAKING ACROSS BORDERS IS NOT LEGAL. THAT MEANS IT'S A CRIME.

Drive across the continental United States.

We got us a big country here. It's full of really cool stuff. We also have the most extensive, complex, and well-maintained system of roads, streets, and highways on the planet. So exploit it—make the most of it, and get out there and hit the open road.

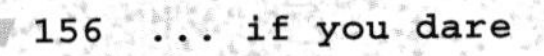

Drive Interstate 70, from Denver to Grand Junction.

You get to go into the mountains, then through the mountains, then down out of the mountains. Try to time it right, though—blizzards often shut down the Eisenhower Tunnel in the winter. And traffic can suck on the weekends. One more thing: Try to remember that every single stretch of road in the world is a potential falling-rock area; the ones with the signs are those places that have already proven to be falling-rock areas. Don't get cocky.

Drive from Frisco to L.A. on the Pacific Coast Highway.

Call it what you will—everybody does. U.S. 1. Cabrillo Highway. Whatever. It's that long, gorgeous stretch of road that is on the left-most boundary of the continental United States. You want to go from north to south, because that way you'll be in the outside lane, looking right out over the water.

329 Drive from Denver to Frisco in thirty hours.

☠ ☠ ☠ ☠ ☠

In the tradition of one of the best of the classic chase films, this one is not easy with modern vehicles and laws.

330 Drive Highway 375 in Nevada.

☠ ☠

What the state now officially calls the "Extraterrestrial Highway," because, well, Nevadans have a wry, cynical side that is quite apt to co-opt any nonsensical goofiness and try to make a buck off it. Supposedly, there are some aliens flying around up there, on a mega-classified Air Force base. Yes. Uh-huh. And supposedly this book will make me a millionaire.

#330

331 Swim in as many oceans/seas/lakes/rivers/large bodies of water as possible.

Check 'em off as you complete each.

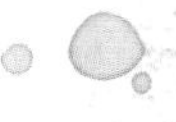

START SIMPLE: SWIM EACH OF THE GREAT LAKES. THEN TRY THE OCEANS. SCATTER YOUR EFFORTS AS MUCH AS POSSIBLE. KEEP A LIST.

332 Take the train from coast to coast.

Your choice: Either latitudinally or longitudinally. Expect frequent, long delays.

333 Ride the rails like a hobo.

I'm not quite sure who the marketing genius was who, over a hundred years ago, implanted in the collective American mind the idea that wandering the land, at the speed of train travel, was a romantic concept. That person should get a medal from the Public Relations Flak Hall of Fame, if such a thing exists. The traditional fantastic motif involves a freight train with a flamboyant name, some fingerless gloves, and a stick holding a satchel made from a knotted kerchief. The real deal involves dirty, cramped conditions and slow, uncomfortable travel.

334 Spend forty-eight hours in a major metropolitan center without a home or hotel.

☠ ☠ ☠

Think of it as an extended travel layover—but don't stay in your port of embarkation; get out and see the city. Walk around. Meet people. Eat in local dives. Drag your belongings with you from place to place. As you start to get really wired, when the lack of sleep starts to fuzz your mind and dawn is yet a few hours away, wander into a small, twenty-four-hour dining establishment of some sort. Make some infrequent, minor purchases until the sun comes back up, and do it again. Stagger into your place of departure on fumes, collapsing into a puddled heap once you finally reach your mode of transportation.

Smuggle something through customs.

This was a lot more fun when we weren't so damned uptight about terrorism, in that brief lull between the highjacking trend in the '60s and '70s and the September 11 attacks. The security staff who work as customs personnel have become really twitchy in virtually every country on the planet.

A SEX TOY IN YOUR LUGGAGE WOULDN'T JUST BE SOMETHING THEY SMIRK AT NOWADAYS.

Smuggle a pet through customs.

A snake will think of you as a big, warm, soft tree (inasmuch as a snake can think, of course). So if you wrap it around your waist, under a bulky sweatshirt, it will stay nice and snug until you get to the other side of the customs area, where you can put it back in your carry-on luggage. No kidding.

337 Circumnavigate the globe.

☠☠☠☠☠

There are several different means to accomplish this: boat, airplane, even—theoretically—by balloon.

TRAVELING THE GLOBE IS NEVER EASY, AND ONLY A FEW PEOPLE IN ALL OF HISTORY HAVE ACCOMPLISHED IT. BE SURE TO PACK A LUNCH.

338 Be a space tourist.

☠☠☠☠☠

Right now, flinging yourself into extra-atmospheric orbit is an extremely expensive proposition, and most of us are unable to avail ourselves of the opportunity. Very soon, though, this should be fairly practical, so why not make a point of accomplishing it.

339 Walk across the downtown area of a major metropolitan city some time after midnight, and before 5 A.M.

☠ ☠ ☠

For some reason, crime and criminals like to congregate in the city center, under cover of darkness. I think this is because (a) that's where all the things and people worth robbing/stealing are located, and (b) nighttime is the traditional occasion for dirty deeds. Hanging out during this period, in this area, is a bad idea. Keep your wits about you.

Cross to the other side of town via the sewer system.

It's been said that a good measure of any civilization is its capacity for removing human waste. By that criterion, America is one damned fine nation—we've got some bee-yoo-ti-ful sewers, and they span far and wide and deep. You can drop down into one without any specific tools or know-how, and wander around for days on end in the labyrinth they form.

BRING SOME HEAVILY SCENTED CREAM FOR YOUR UPPER LIP.

Live in the Manhattan sewer system for a week.

Supposedly, there are colonies of vagrants nestled down there, with an extensive warren of hidey-holes and a rudimentary society built from primitive gibberish. And crocodiles.

 Visit the embassy of a foreign country.

☠

They might feed you exotic cuisine, native to the nation the embassy represents, such as falafel, dolmes, or Coca-Cola and potato chips. You may meet dignitaries, or embassy staffers, diplomats trained to communicate with Americans in our own peculiar mode of conversation (brash, loud, and overly personal).

 Visit your own embassy while traveling abroad.

☠ ☠ ☠

Just leaving our country will make you appreciate it more. But going to one of our embassies while in a foreign country will let you see how much other people really appreciate our country, too. Even in a country with a government and population that purports to hate Americans, there is usually a long line of people waiting eagerly to get inside and make their pitch for a visa. One of the best feelings in the world, the warmest sort of camaraderie, is when those Marine guards wave you past the line and right inside because you have that blue (or green) passport with an eagle on the front of it.

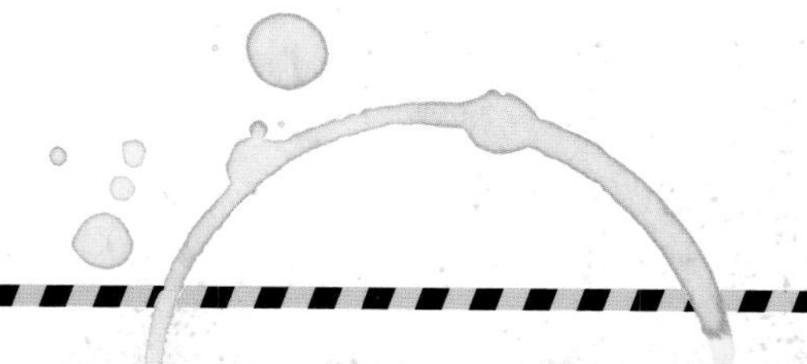

Have sex in all fifty states.

☠☠☠

It's good to have goals. Plus, it's one great excuse to get out and see this country of ours.

IT CAN BE SOMEWHAT CHALLENGING TO COME UP WITH REASONS TO GO TO SOME OF OUR STATES. THAT'S PART OF THE FUN, TOO.

Have sex with the same partner in all fifty states.

☠☠☠☠

Now you've doubled the complexity of the thing. Yowza.

346 Go to Colombia.

☠☠☠☠☠

Gorgeous land, friendly people, terrific food, great prices. In the words of my closest friend: "If they would just get their political act together, this would be a great tourist destination."

347 Hit Amsterdam.

☠ ☠ ☠

Yeah, there's the stuff with the Red Light District, and the drug bars, and the beer—but they also have . . . good food. The foreign restaurants, I mean. Dutch food pretty much sucks.

348 Visit Anne Frank's house.

☠ ☠ ☠

Okay, it's not really Anne's house; it's the house where she stayed while hiding from Nazis and writing her book. It's a powerful place to be—to see just where she was, and get a feel for the size of the place.

349 Go to the Middle East.

☠ ☠ ☠ ☠ ☠

See what all the shouting is about. Then leave as soon as possible.

350 Go to Jerusalem.

☠☠☠☠☠

See the city people are willing to kill and die for.

351 Go to Mecca during the pilgrimage.

☠☠☠☠☠

Throngs of people, crowded together, sharing a religious experience. Sort of like New Orleans during Mardi Gras, without the alcohol, sex, or fun.

352 Visit a no-kidding Scottish castle.

Learn that castle life was probably not nearly as romantic as we like to think it was. And all that nonsense about who had what scepter, or where the actual crown was, and what royal ass was planted on which rock. . . . Very, very silly, to contemporary minds. But I guess they didn't have television back then, and needed something to talk about.

353 Drive a car in Great Britain.

Pure, unadulterated misery.

354 Visit Japan.

There is something absolutely infuriating about people who smile politely when they have no idea what you're trying to communicate to them. I think it has to do with an American inferiority complex, in that we think we're being laughed at, when we just really want to get to the bathroom.

VISITING JAPAN IS DARING NOT ONLY FOR THE CULTURAL SHOCK, BUT THE EXPENSE AND DISTANCE.

Stay in a hotel.

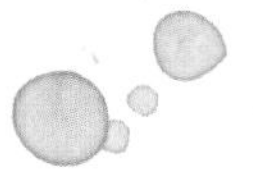

☠

It's a place that you don't own, usually comprised solely of a bedroom, where you get to sleep in exchange for a rental fee. The place exists for just this purpose, which means others have stayed in the room before you, and others will stay in the room after you've left.

MANY HAVE ALREADY STAYED IN YOUR ROOM. TRY NOT TO THINK ABOUT WHAT THAT MEANS ABOUT THE BEDDING. . . .

Stay in a crummy hotel.

☠☠☠

Surprisingly, the pay-by-the-hour, no-tell motels are not the biggest fleabags, in my experience. As a matter of fact, the worst place I ever stayed in was not a $15-per-hour room in the back streets of a metropolitan city, but a hotel that belongs to a major hotel chain, located in rural Indiana. The floor was matted with filth, the various amenity fixtures (such as lighting and heat) didn't work, and I was forced to kill not one but two crickets who had made themselves at home between the wall and the air conditioner. Not the best night's sleep on record.

357 Stay in a five-star hotel.

☠ ☠ ☠

True, the rooms may compare unfavorably with their $60-a-night counterparts, but what makes the difference (and what you're really paying for at these places) is the service, which is almost uniformly superb.

358 Stay at an all-inclusive resort.

☠ ☠ ☠

The kind of place where your payment covers not only your room, but food and entertainment as well. These are touted as the end-all, be-all of travel luxury, but can be close to a rip-off if you don't inspect the value. Make sure your alcoholic beverages are included in the price, as that's where you're going to make up a lot of the differential in cost.

#358

359 Visit Death Valley.

☠ ☠ ☠

This is one of the hottest, driest, lowest places on Earth (of course, it's in California, where hospitality is at a premium). Do not stay long. Heck, if you can swing it, don't even get out of your vehicle.

360 Drive through Death Valley during the springtime bloom.

☠ ☠ ☠

Strangely, if enough rain falls on the region during winter, an amazing amount and variety of wildflowers bloom in April or May. This is very impressive. Take lots of water.

361 Do New York City.

☠☠☠☠

Thousands of years from now, historians will goggle at the complexity and vastness of the city rising from the tiny island and its outlying areas. They will mention it in reverent tones, eliciting the same reactions we currently feel when we hear the names "Thebes," "Troy," "Babylon," and "Atlantis." Granted, they will not have known how expensive, dirty, and full of New Yorkers it was, or how vastly overrated were its attractions.

NEW YORK IS THE CURRENT PINNACLE OF HUMAN EXISTENCE, SO YOU HAVE TO DO IT AT LEAST ONCE.

362 Check out Chicago.

☠☠☠

There's lots to do in the most frantic of Midwestern cities. But please, please, please, whatever you do, don't go there in winter (i.e., any months that aren't July or August).

363 Cross any red line painted on the ground of a property owned by the Department of Defense.

☠☠☠☠☠

Here's the deal: that red line is the demarcation between areas where you are—nominally—allowed to traverse freely, and those where you are most certainly not allowed to move about. Military people do not take kindly to people who are "breaking red." It's not a good thing to do. They will let you know this. Most often, they will let you know this while you are facedown on the pavement, with the barrel of a firearm pressed behind your ear, and a knee in the small of your back.

THOSE GUARDS MAY DECIDE TO SHOOT FIRST AND ASK QUESTIONS LATER, WHICH IS THEIR PREROGATIVE.

364 Break into a secure facility.

☠☠☠

The easiest way to do this is to walk right in, during business hours, pretending like you belong there. Carry a clipboard, and before someone notices you and walks up to ask what the hell you're doing, walk up to them and tell them to take you wherever it is you want to go. Oh, this is probably a federal offense.

365 Visit an active nuclear reactor.

☠☠

In actuality, nuclear reactors are extremely safe mechanisms; there's plenty of shielding and security and whatnot. It's the radioactive fuel that's the scary thing. But most of that is locked up pretty well, and they're fairly careful with it. So go check it out. Tell me about it when you get back.

366 Explore a geographic area undiscovered or rarely visited by any other human beings.

☠☠☠☠☠

The real tough part is finding a place like that left on our planet. Once there, be really careful, because you don't quite know what is fatal to humans, yet.

NATURE THINGS Our species has gone to great lengths to distance ourselves from nature. With cause: nature is a nasty, ugly thing, where living creatures die quite readily, in a variety of ways. So one great source of Things is the sensation of being present for a demonstration of one of nature's bitchier habits. Inland, you've got tornadoes and earthquakes. On the coasts, you've got typhoons, hurricanes, and tidal waves. Everywhere, you've got mudslides, sinkholes, huge hail, lightning, and temperatures that fluctuate rapidly enough to freeze or fry a human. Take your raincoat.

367 Look into an active volcano.

☠☠☠

There are over a thousand volcanoes on this planet. Go find one and check it out—tell the rest of us what it's like, will ya?

368 Flee a lahar.

☠☠☠☠☠

Lahar is a mixture of water and pieces of rock, flowing away from volcanoes, or in river valleys. Basically, this stuff takes on the consistency of wet cement and moves pretty darned fast—faster than lava, even.

LAHARS CAN ALSO BE HUNDREDS OF FEET WIDE, AND CARRY BIG HONKING BOULDERS WITH THEM.

 Outrun a lava flow.

☠☠☠☠☠

According to official government sources, lava can travel at speeds greater than 30 kilometers per hour, if channeled and moving downhill. Before unraveling the real mystery here, realize that you can't reasonably move that fast for any length of time. Of course, there are different kinds of lava, some more viscous than others. Not that you want to check the viscosity of the stuff before deciding whether or not to leave the area. Duh.

 Survive a tephra shower.

☠☠☠☠–☠☠☠☠☠, depending on conditions

You know how volcanoes can blow stuff up into the air? That stuff is called tephra, and it includes both molten and solid rock. That stuff has to come down, too, via gravity. You don't really want to be under it when it does.

371 Experience an earthquake.

☠ – ☠☠☠☠☠, depending on conditions

When the very ground you're on starts to shake, accompanied by a significant rumbling, it's easy to leap to the conclusion that something just exploded, or that someone is dropping bombs on you. Even if you anticipated the natural occurrence, it is still unsettling. Especially if you're trying to walk at the time.

372 Experience a hurricane.

☠ – ☠☠☠☠☠, depending on conditions

The tornado's coast-dwelling cousin, the hurricane can make the dirt-bound funnel seem tame in comparison. In addition to the horrific winds, you get the full benefit of nature at its most malicious: deadly storms, floods, and huge waves inundating the area.

373 Experience a tornado.

☠ – ☠☠☠☠☠, depending on conditions

Kids growing up in the Midwest get an education in an eerily Cold War–type survival technique: the duck-and-cover-'cause-a-tornado's-coming tactic. It's difficult to imagine that a force of nature will somehow be dissuaded from destroying you because you're cowering in a ditch or against a wall, but who knows? It might work. When you see the sky turn a dark, sickly green, and there's a creepy stillness amidst a summer storm, it's quite possible one of those brutal funnel clouds is about to touch down and wreak havoc. Best to avoid trailer parks in that situation.

374 Experience an avalanche.

☠ – ☠☠☠☠☠, depending on conditions

Tons of ice, rock, and assorted debris falling at terminal velocity from elevation. It's going to stop when it wants to stop, and there's not a damned thing you can do about it (assuming, of course, we can anthropomorphize an inimical natural occurrence).

AVALANCHES ARE PROBABLY BEST WITNESSED STANDING TO THE SIDE OR ABOVE THE POINT AT WHICH THEY ORIGINATE, AS OPPOSED TO ANYWHERE BELOW. . . .

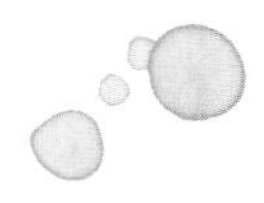

375 Experience a mudslide.

☠ – ☠☠☠☠☠, depending on conditions

The avalanche's junior partner, a mudslide can be just as deadly and destructive. Usually found in hilly areas where poor construction and land maintenance, combined with heavy rainfall, has led to serious erosion.

IF YOU THINK DROWNING IS BAD, TRY IMAGINING DROWNING IN MUD.

376 Experience a sinkhole.

☠ – ☠☠☠☠☠, depending on conditions

Sort of a reverse-mudslide, the sinkhole can vary in speed and degree. Basically, the ground opens up to swallow anything on the surface; it can be a sudden implosion, or a gradual, creeping spread of the hole's perimeter, ceasing only when subterranean architecture is totally exposed. Not a fun place to be, for the most part.

377 Experience a tidal wave (tsunami).

☠ – ☠☠☠☠☠, depending on conditions

This is a massive, crushing power, capable of obliterating just about anything along the coast, and can carry destruction well inland. If you can manage it, be airborne at the time.

378 Experience serious hail.

☠ – ☠☠☠☠☠, depending on conditions

As opposed to regular hail, which isn't quite as scary. Serious hail can come in three configurations: freakishly large hail, a dramatic amount of hail, or a combination of the two.

379 Experience a flood.

☠ – ☠☠☠☠☠, depending on conditions

Sudden inundation with water is a fear harbored by our species for thousands of years—with good reason. Anything from the urban peril of clogged runoff drains (the ominous "flash-flooding") to the rural deluge can wash away homes, vehicles, and certainly people. Be sure you know how to swim—that's just basic.

380 Experience lightning.

☠ – ☠ ☠ ☠ ☠ ☠, depending on conditions

Don't just sit on your front porch in the middle of July and gaze out comfortably at the beautiful display of heat lightning. Get out into some quasi-wilderness in the middle of a bitchin' storm and know what it's really like to see lightning nail something in dramatic fashion. Just hope it isn't you.

381 Let a really big, hairy spider walk across your body.

☠ ☠ ☠ – ☠ ☠ ☠ ☠ ☠, depending on species

Pick any of the nasty (or nasty-looking) ones: a tarantula, a Sydney funnel-web, a Brazilian wanderer. . . . Feel those spiny hairs tickle your skin? See its globulous eye cluster? Everything in your body recoils at just the sight of it. So why are you touching it? Oh, and some of them are deadly.

382 Pet a porcupine.

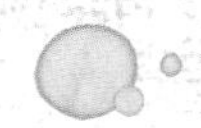

This is like those little security blades in the driveways of some parking lots: If you drive over them in one direction, you're fine, but they'll slash your tires to pieces if you go the other way. A porcupine is nature's parking-lot-blade-thing.

PET A PORCUPINE IN ONE DIRECTION, YOU'RE OKAY; IT'S NOT SOFT OR FLUFFY OR ANYTHING—BUT IN THE OTHER DIRECTION, WELL....

383 Feed a wallaby.

Yeah, they look just like cute miniature kangaroos, don't they? And, as we all know from a formative diet of Saturday-morning television programming, kangaroos are sweet, adorable, nice animals. So as you reach over the fence to offer a handful of Wallaby Kibble to a waiting marsupial, you will probably be quite shocked when it grabs the cuff of your sleeve, yanks you, jabs you a couple of times, and bites your palm. I know I was.

384 Milk a cow.

☠☠☠

Okay, if you've been to a dairy farm, then this isn't such a big deal.

MOST OF THE MODERN AMERICAN POPULACE HAS NEVER BEEN TO A DAIRY FARM AND DON'T REALIZE THAT COWS CAN STEP ON PEOPLE QUITE EASILY. OR KICK THEM.

385 Get stung by a bee.

☠ – ☠☠☠☠☠, depending on circumstances

It's an annoying, painful sensation that can raise a welt and irritate you for hours. Unless you're one of those who are horribly allergic to such afflictions—in which case, you might die.

386 Encounter a wolf.

☠☠☠☠

A family I knew in Colorado was licensed to keep wolves on their property. I was on their patio one night, looking into the woods, with one of the family members with me. One second there was nothing there—the next, there were three pairs of red eyes staring at me, in a staggered line about twenty yards across. I was told to stay immobile, but the command wasn't necessary: While something deep in the recesses of my brain was screaming, "Shouldn't be here. Should be anywhere but here," my body was doing its best to shut down all ambulatory functions. Harrowing.

Look at the sun during an eclipse.

☠ ☠ – ?, depending on who you believe

Supposedly, this is bad for you. I am not quite sure how. Like, radiation, or something. Back in grade school, they made us build this weird cardboard eclipse-viewing thing, and warned us repeatedly not to look at the sun directly. They made it sound very dangerous. This was repeated to the point that it sounded so drastic that, if you failed to heed the warning, your eyes would melt and drip down your face, or your skull would explode, or your hair would catch on fire or something. So, of course, I did it. I currently retain 20/15 vision in both eyes. Maybe from looking at eclipses.

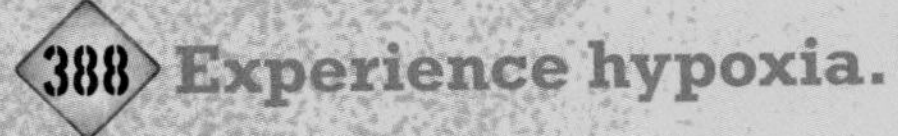

388 Experience hypoxia.

☠☠☠☠☠

Up at high altitudes, the air is rare—not much oxygen, the go-juice for human life. This can occur in high-flying aircraft, and the conditions can be simulated with a hyperbaric chamber. When the brain doesn't get enough oxygen, it does funny things. Your fine motor skills start to deteriorate, and your judgment follows. Pretty soon, you're feeling drunk and goofy, and you seriously consider voting for whoever makes the best campaign promises. This can be deadly if you don't get some oxygen soon.

389 Experience nitrogen narcosis.

☠☠☠☠☠

If you're going to scuba, especially to any considerable depth (thirty meters or deeper), you should familiarize yourself with the risks and effects of this condition, as well as recognition of its symptoms. For some reason, nitrogen under high pressure (the main component of the air in your tanks) makes the human nervous system do some bizarre things: you can start to feel drunk, or elated, or extremely paranoid. Yes, it does sound like someone slipping you bad drugs at a rave—but you're deep under water, and the consequences of any irresponsible actions can be fatal.

Experience the "bends."

☠☠☠☠☠

The opposite cause of nitrogen narcosis: if you're scuba-diving, and come up too quickly, the compressed nitrogen which is usually absorbed by the body's tissues instead converts to tiny bubbles in the bloodstream. These get lodged in the tight corners, nooks, and crannies of the human body, which usually occur at the joints. This malady is not limited to divers; it can occur in anyone who moves rapidly from one environment to another with much less pressure, including people in pressurized mineshafts and those who fly in aircraft with unpressurized cabins.

BAD THINGS CAN HAPPEN BECAUSE OF THE BENDS, EVERYTHING FROM SKIN RASHES TO SHARP PAINS TO DEATH.

Survive a venereal disease.

☠☠☠–☠☠☠☠☠, depending on circumstances

Ahem. Yes. Well. In this, as in several other Things, the treatment can be somewhat worse than the malady.

392 Build a campfire.

☠ – ☠ ☠ ☠, depending on circumstances

Open flames are not only dangerous, but they're also fascinating on a primordial level. Do your best to conduct this practice in a safe manner: have a source of fire-damping material (water, sand, etc.) nearby, know the wind direction and speed, and build it with sufficient firebreaks.

393 Build a campfire without using modern tools or accelerants.

☠ ☠ ☠ ☠

There are several methods for this: the ol' rubbing-sticks-together, flint and steel, etc. None of them is easy. Get in touch with your inner Neanderthal.

#393

394 Engage in naked fire-jumping.

☠ ☠ ☠ ☠

Those who have told me of this practice explain that there is a quasi-tribal cathartic thrill, probably a result of the instantaneous liberation from social conventions. I'm thinking beer was involved.

395 Throw a disposable lighter into a fire.

☠ ☠ ☠ ☠ ☠

Once that fuel heats up, inside that little container, the flammable gas wants to force its way out of constraint, in any way possible.

ONCE THE LIGHTER'S SHELL MELTS OR IS CRACKED, ALL THAT FUEL, USUALLY IN GASEOUS FORM, IS GOING TO DETONATE. DRAMATICALLY. STAND WAY, WAY BACK.

396 Run from a dog.

☠ ☠ ☠

With the low center of gravity, four legs, and thousands of generations behind it, the dog is perfectly bred for chasing you. You, with your two spindly little legs and head bobbing way above the ground, are not designed to outrun anything. Try, anyway.

397 Intervene in a dogfight.

☠☠☠☠

Not the brightest of ideas; a dog, in the midst of a battle, will flail about with its teeth and jaws, trying to bite pretty much anything. This means that even if you are trying to salvage your own pet, you are as likely to get bitten by it as by its opponent.

BEST TO TRY SOME OTHER METHOD, SUCH AS HOSING BOTH DOGS DOWN WITH COLD WATER, FROM A SAFE DISTANCE.

398 Kill the last remaining member of a species.

☠☠☠☠☠

It might taste good.

399 Survive a disease.

☠ – ☠☠☠☠☠, depending on circumstances

Of all the big things that can smash you (rocks, gravity, vehicles, etc.), it's pretty amazing that few of them are as uniformly lethal as microbes, the tiny little buggers that can get inside your body and lay you out fast. Disease has killed far more people than any other cause, including warfare. Rest, and get plenty of fluids.

SUPERSTITIOUS THINGS Sometimes, violating the precepts of a superstition/urban legend/old wives' tale is one of the most difficult things we can do; the social mores of the society we were raised in are a stringent motivator, even if we know better. So just go ahead and try something you know to be rooted in a ridiculous, nonsensical belief; nothing bad is going to happen to you. Well, most likely.

400 Go swimming less than a half-hour after a meal.

☠ ☠

It's not clear why someone suggested that this practice be prohibited. . . . Something to do with muscle cramps, probably, but why would ingestion be linked to muscular performance? Of course, doing any exercise on a full stomach can be a bit nauseating, and forceful vomiting while immersed in open water could be dangerous, so try to keep your food down.

401 Stay overnight in a house/cave/room/building said to be "haunted."

That place in Amityville. Alcatraz. The Bunnyman Bridge in Virginia.

402 Start your own religion.

Most of the world's religions claim to say much the same thing as the others—they all lie. They all say something incredibly distinct, and they all want you to pay homage to their archaic methods and concepts. So be an individual, flaunt tradition, and become a heretic. Proselytize.

403 Swallow your gum.

Sure, someone once said that it messes with your digestive system. Whatever. Go ahead and swallow it, just to show them.

404 Survive a curse.

☠

Let someone curse you, then make it a daily practice to call the curser on the telephone and announce the fact that you're still quite alive.

THE POWER OF THE HUMAN MIND IS AMAZING—IF YOU ACTUALLY BELIEVE YOU ARE GOING TO DIE, IT'S POSSIBLE YOU'LL TALK YOURSELF INTO BEING A CORPSE.

405 Debunk an urban legend.

☠

You've got that friend/family member/dipshit coworker/acquaintance—you know the one. The one who keeps forwarding you stupid crap they've received via e-mail. Go surf over to *www.snopes.com* and find the page outlining how this particular stupidity is ridiculous. Copy and paste the link, and send it back. If he or she was churlish enough to include every recipient's e-mail address, use Reply to All, and let everyone know how goofy the sender is. Hopefully, a little public humiliation will quell the e-mailer's desire to continue the practice.

406 Throw a hat on a bed.

☠

In some superstitious circles, this will result in something bad happening to you.

UNLESS YOU HAVE LICE, WHAT ILL EFFECT MIGHT SPRING FROM THROWING A HAT ON THE BED?

407 Walk under a ladder.

☠ ☠

Who knows how refraining from this became superstition instead of simply remaining "a good way to avoid being bonked on the noggin by stuff dropped by whoever's on the ladder." But whatever—it's your Thing.

408 Step on a crack.

☠

Nobody's spine will suffer the slightest damage, I assure you.

409 Shower during a thunderstorm.

Common knowledge has it that any stray lightning bolt that connects with your domicile while you are in the shower will course through your plumbing and use your body to complete the circuit, frying you like so much chicken. Common knowledge, of course, is largely comprised of stupidity spouted by morons. Go ahead and get clean, no matter what the weather is like.

410 Use a homemade contraceptive device or method.

I had a friend who once tried to convince me that his utilization of plastic cling wrap was a great idea. I tried, momentarily, to disabuse him of his misplaced pride in innovation. It didn't work. I think his girlfriend ended up preggers. Boy, was I surprised.

Part 2: Private Things

Some things are exciting, yet not for the prying eyes of others. And there are some Things that just can't involve others, for a variety of reasons (including good taste and nowhere to comfortably place your elbows). So go ahead and take the plunge—but keep 'em to yourself.

MISCELLANEOUS THINGS There are those Things that don't fit neatly into other categories. This makes them no less fun or challenging, however. Take a look and see what you might like.

411 Feed a live animal to a snake.

☠☠

Sure, a snake will eat pithed food—I've even known people who kept snake treats in the freezer. But that's plainly unnatural, and unfair to the snake. The snake wants something fresh, like it was evolved to eat. And there are few things as fascinating as watching that timeless death-dance.

412 Blow something up with explosives.

☠☠☠☠

Explosives are nasty, despicable things. This is because, unlike projectile weapons, they are utterly indiscriminate. Oh, sure, there are nifty adaptations like shaped charges, but explosives really just comply with one set of rules: high school physics.

A GUN, YOU CAN POINT. EXPLOSIVES? JUST BE OUT OF THE WAY. WAY OUT OF THE WAY.

413 Use dynamite.

☠☠☠☠☠

This practice has a lot more to do with the fuse and the blasting cap than with the explosive itself. Still, it seems awful risky. Be very careful.

414 Undertake a hands-on project involving a field you know nothing about, have no training in, harbor no inclinations for, and generally dislike.

☠☠☠

Try something in the field of automotive repair, plumbing, carpentry, metalworking, computer networking, etc. Do the best job you can.

415 Build a house.

☠☠☠☠☠

Pretty much the ultimate in the Handiwork Department. If you can put together a human dwelling, you're certainly ahead of most of the global population.

416 Build a house you intend to live in yourself.

☠ ☠ ☠ ☠ ☠

There's the true test of your belief in your work. A poorly constructed domicile can kill you in so many, many ways.

417 Use a power tool.

☠ ☠ – ☠ ☠ ☠ ☠ ☠, depending on conditions

The tool doesn't care what it's working on. Be it concrete, wood, metal, or human flesh, the tool will keep on doing whatever it's designed to do, unless it's switched off or loses power.

418 Spend a winter in Wisconsin.

☠☠☠

Yeah, that stinging feeling in your eyes? It's your tears starting to freeze in their ducts. Snowfall here is a lot different than in any non-Midwestern state.

IN WISCONSIN, IF SIX FEET OF SNOW FALL OVERNIGHT, MCDONALD'S MIGHT CLOSE, BUT THOSE SCHOOL BUSES ARE RUNNING.

419 Spend a summer in Mississippi.

☠☠☠

There are a lot of unfair stereotypes made about Mississippi, about the people there, about the social mores, about the weather. Most of it is deserved. Some of the best food you'll ever eat, though. Wash it down with cold beer and try not to sweat too much.

420 Run with scissors.

☠☠☠☠

Why do you think that every parent/teacher/grownup in the world told you not to do this all those years?

421 Adopt a pet from an animal shelter.

☠☠☠☠

This is more dangerous than buying a used car; you're getting somebody else's problems, just like a used animal. But the worst thing a car will do is kill you, which is over quickly. You might fall in love with your new pet, and then realize too late that you'll have to put it to sleep because it's got a fatal disease, and then you're worse off than before—now you've got a big pet-shaped hole in your life, and no pet.

422 Steal something.

☠☠☠☠

I swiped a corncob pipe (retail price: thirty-five cents) from Swan's Pharmacy when I was six years old. My tiny prepubescent body exuded more sweat than it had in my entire life up until that point. What a rush. And I still feel guilty to this day.

Steal something of great value.

☠☠☠☠

The jewels of an heiress. A foreign sports car. A vast amount of wealth in an incredibly liquid form, such as paper currency. Gold. It's called grand larceny, and it makes for good movies—but can you pull it off? Probably not.

Hotwire a car.

☠☠☠

This is a really cool skill to have, just in case, you know, you misplace your car keys and don't have a Triple-A membership.

WITH MODERN VEHICLES, HOTWIRING IS AN INCREDIBLY COMPLEX AND DIFFICULT ACHIEVEMENT. MIGHT AS WELL GO GET A DEGREE IN ELECTRONIC ENGINEERING.

Reformat your hard drive.

☠☠☠☠

You've got information you've been saving for years. Aunt Eustace's address. The lifetime warranty number for your brake pads. All those URLs in your Favorites folder. Precious stuff, indeed. So back it up, carefully, and wipe your machine to start from scratch. Good luck.

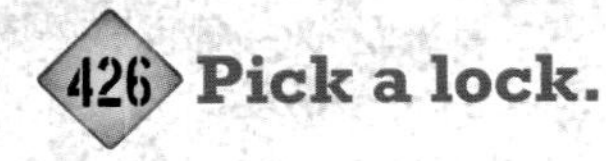

426 Pick a lock.

Locks, oddly, aren't as hard to defeat as you might imagine; they just take a little bit of time and perseverance, combined with a modicum of manual dexterity.

PICK ONE OF YOUR OWN LOCKS, AS ATTEMPTING THIS ON SOMEONE ELSE'S MAY RESULT IN A RATHER LONG JAIL STINT.

427 Mix household cleaners.

There are infinite ways to combine, collect, and coagulate all sorts of nifty chemicals, using stuff you buy off the shelf at the supermarket or hardware store. They can give you some funky results, too, like napalm, mustard gas, or chemical explosives. Much fun can ensue (if you don't kill yourself). You won't find any formulas in this book: There are other books (and the Internet) for that. Kids, don't try this at home. Or anywhere else you might get caught.

428 Look down the barrel of a loaded gun.

☠☠☠☠☠

There are few things more shock-dumb terrifying. If it ever happens, you may find yourself suddenly focused entirely on that single point in space, or you may find your mind wandering to other, totally unrelated ambient occurrences, such as what the air happens to smell like at the moment. Not a comforting sensation.

429 Put your fist through a wall.

☠☠☠

It's one of those childish displays of angry immaturity, striking out vindictively, trying to punish only yourself and an inanimate object. Feel better?

RELATIONSHIP THINGS Love is the source of the most irrational behavior. Therefore, monkeying with it may be the most foolhardy thing you can do.

430 Tell someone close to you that you find their opinions utterly reprehensible.

☠ ☠ ☠ ☠

You want the fastest way to ensure that something will always be haunting your relationship, something known but unsaid for the rest of the time you know each other? Try this.

431 Flirt.

☠ ☠

Check out that cutie over there. Throw a wink, a nod. Smile at the person serving you food, and chat them up a little. Start something. Get a phone number or e-mail address. This is, of course, all sorts of troubling, for a variety of reasons. You could enrage a devoted significant other/admirer of the target of your flirtation, and they could choose to do you bodily harm. Dangerous fun.

MAYBE YOU ONLY INTENDED TO BE FRIENDLY, AND THE RECIPIENT TOOK YOUR FLIRTING AS A ROMANTIC OVERTURE, AND WILL NOW BE HURT BY THE MISUNDERSTANDING.

432 Flirt with someone whose significant other is present.

☠ ☠ ☠

Okay. Okay. The only way to be cool and do this is when there are two couples present, and everyone's a friend of everyone else, and they all understand you're just joking. So do it that way. Anything else, and you're just a jerk.

433 Flirt with someone for the express purpose of getting something you want.

☠ ☠ ☠

Some people find this inappropriate. Maybe they're bad flirters. Or unattractive. Or both.

434 Give your significant other general power of attorney.

☠☠☠☠☠

Marriage? Cliché. Diamonds? Useless, overpriced rocks, product of a perfect marketing/con job. This is the sure way to find out whether or not that other person is truly in love with you, or whether he or she is just wheedling to find a way to screw you royally. It can also be the express train to Doomed City. Enjoy the trip.

435 Ask your partner for a prenup.

☠☠☠☠

Want to really test the durability of your relationship? Asking for a three-way is passé. Having an affair is trite, and minuscule in comparison. Go ahead and ask your love-buddy to put their assertions of undying love and fealty down on paper. Be prepared to duck.

436 Get divorced.

☠☠☠☠☠+

Look, make it easier on yourself: Drink drain cleaner, stick a large magnum handgun in your mouth, then slip a plastic bag over your head and tie it off with a nylon noose. There's no reason to even mess around with this one—pure suicide. Did you know some people do this more than once? They never survive, though.

DATING THINGS The ancient mating ritual. The human courter approaches the target tangentially, as if careless of the need for affection, pretending to be blasé—the target acts in the same manner. Somehow, they're supposed to end up in bed. Weird.

437 Make a pass at an incredibly attractive stranger.

☠ ☠ ☠ ☠

Really attractive people are constantly hit on, often by people with far more to offer than you ever possibly could. Odds are almost certain that you will be shot down, and quite likely in a completely humiliating way.

WHAT HAVE YOU GOT TO LOSE WHEN MAKING A PASS BUT SOME SELF-RESPECT? NO GUTS, NO GLORY.

438 Break up with someone.

☠ – ☠ ☠ ☠ ☠, depending on circumstances

This can be incredibly painful, and far more devastating than many of the physical dangers posed by some of the Things in this book. More often, however, it's an awkward relief, one for which you might feel guilty. In that case, recognize it for what it is: a damned smart move—you should have gotten out earlier.

439 Tell someone you've had a crush on for a long time how you feel.

☠ ☠

Just because it seems like every other movie suggests that is a bad idea. "Bad" in the sense that you will never have the relationship you once had with that person. Good, in the sense that you can stop wasting time being his or her emotional crutch and constant suck-up, because the object of your desire is not going to deal with you anymore. Congrats for that.

440 Tell a first date you're only interested in kinky sex.

☠ ☠ ☠ ☠ ☠

If you're on a first date, that means the other person already digs you to some extent. Springing a kink on them will do two things: save you a lot of time waiting to get around to asking them once you've already established a relationship, and, on very rare occasions, pleasantly surprise the other person, who just so happens to have that same kink.

© istockphoto.com / Martin-Carlsson

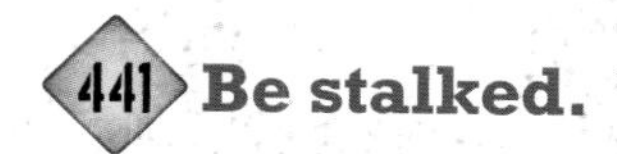

441 Be stalked.

☠ ☠ ☠

There is nothing quite as flattering as having your very own stalker. Of course, there's nothing quite as spooky, either.

BEING STALKED STOPS BEING FUN REAL FAST, SO MAKE THE MOST OF IT WHILE YOU CAN—BEFORE YOU'RE FORCED TO CALL THE AUTHORITIES.

442 Stalk someone.

☠ ☠ ☠ ☠

No, it's not cool. No, it's not romantic. No, it's not sweet. It's ugly, and, depending on your jurisdiction, probably illegal.

443 Perform a ridiculously romantic stunt, the kind that would normally only be done by a fictional character, in the hopes of impressing a prospective partner.

☠ – ☠ ☠ ☠ ☠ ☠, depending on circumstances

Er—in reality, this usually only results in the target of your ardor being incredibly weirded-out by your mode of advance. Or with you in jail. This is why the behavior is mainly limited to fictional characters.

BEDROOM THINGS Americans are prudes. More so than just about any other group in the history of the planet, American prudishness makes us hypocritical and nauseating. Which can add a nice zing to a Thing.

444 Take your significant other to a strip club.

This can be uncomfortable. . . . It's sometimes tough to see the object of your affection drooling over someone else, right in front of you. But that's okay—it's sometimes tough for them, too. It is good to remember, though, that your partner is a sexual being, and has still chosen to hang out with you most of the time.

445 Have a one-night stand.

Tales of the '70s have made their way down through the generations. Supposedly, that mythic world offered promises of freaky sex, with an endless stream of willing partners, low risk of pregnancy, and simple diseases that could be treated with a few hypodermic shots.

ONE-NIGHT STANDS ARE NOW THE TYPE OF DANGEROUS ACTIVITY AKIN TO DIVING NAKED WITH SHARKS AND AN OPEN WOUND.

446 Try a three-way where both additional participants are of a gender you're attracted to.

This is the brass ring—the big one. The wildly bestest of them all. Be warned however: There may be a downside, especially if you're conducting this experiment with someone you care about. There is always the chance of jealousy complicating things. Moreover, this is reality, where the sights and sounds and tactile sensations involve actual people—so it won't feel like a porno, either during or after.

447 Sleep with a coworker.

Everybody says how stupid and dangerous this is. Amazingly, they're actually correct. There is absolutely no good way to pull this off. You shouldn't try. Although, according to one recent survey, about half of Americans do.

Join the Mile-High Club.

Yes. Sex in an aircraft at altitude. You are not the first to think of it. It's also probably a federal offense, depending on the attitude of the flight crew who catch you.

Have sex in your workplace.

Unless you're in the sex trade, this is definitely expressly forbidden. Also, conducting this activity will most likely involve at least one other Thing. Just about everybody thinks about this; we all think it will be fun and kooky.

LIKE MOST OTHER ADVENTUROUS SEX, WORKPLACE MATING IS BOUND TO BE MORE COMPLICATED AND UNCOMFORTABLE THAN IN YOUR FANTASY.

Have an affair with a married person.

This is one of those clinically dumb activities usually enjoyed by younger people who don't know any better, or older people who don't care. It's also steeped in an unrealistic attraction of the forbidden. That wears off about the third time you have to go out a window with no pants.

451 Have sex in a moving vehicle.

☠☠☠

Not nearly as enjoyable or simple as you'd think. In addition to the problems concerning space, privacy, and logistics, there is the hazard of traffic (pedestrian or otherwise).

452 Have sex with an inanimate object.

☠ – ☠☠☠, depending on circumstances

Thousands of urban legends surround this practice. Maybe you can start one.

453 Have sex in public.

☠☠

Usually, we like to have privacy in which to get on with our freak. Usually. But sometimes, having a bit of the thrill of being "caught" by others adds a little zing. Sometimes.

454 Engage in mate-swapping.

☠☠☠☠

There's an entire American mythos surrounding this practice, steeped in mystique. Actually, it's a great way to ruin all sorts of relationships. Couples that can pull this off—and remain couples—are extremely rare.

Have sex in the shower.

☠☠☠

Something about watery escapades makes them extremely torrid and exciting. If you don't deplete all the hot water, that is. Nothing worse than cold water to, well, throw cold water on the situation. Plus, anything watery has the additional detriment of rinsing away lubrication. Tricky.

YOU WILL NEED SOME BALANCE FOR SHOWER SEX. A WELL-PLACED TOWEL RACK CAN MAKE ALL THE DIFFERENCE.

Have sex in a swimming pool.

☠☠☠

Not just water, but cold, chlorinated water. Hmmmm . . . no.

Have a surreptitious affair.

☠☠☠☠

Er . . . so you're supposed to be in a monogamous arrangement . . . but there's this other person. . . . Well, what is the trite aphorism? "Illicit indulgences are really good in bed," or something? You're going to have to find out for yourself. And keep it on the down-low.

IDEOLOGICAL/PHILOSOPHICAL/INTELLECTUAL THINGS As adults, we're fairly convinced that our way of thinking is correct; it's gotten us this far, at least. We're set in our ways. Things that don't fit in our worldview, or things that contradict what we believe, are tossed away as useless or wrong. This series of Things might be the most difficult, then—these are things that might make you re-examine your perspective, or even change the way you think, which can be very uncomfortable until you get used to the new modes of thought.

458 Read a book that you were supposed to read in high school or college, but found way too boring.

☠ ☠ ☠

Really make it difficult: pick something written by Proust, Dostoyevsky, or Dickens. Ultimate challenge: pick a ludicrously long book, like *Moby Dick* or *War and Peace*.

#458

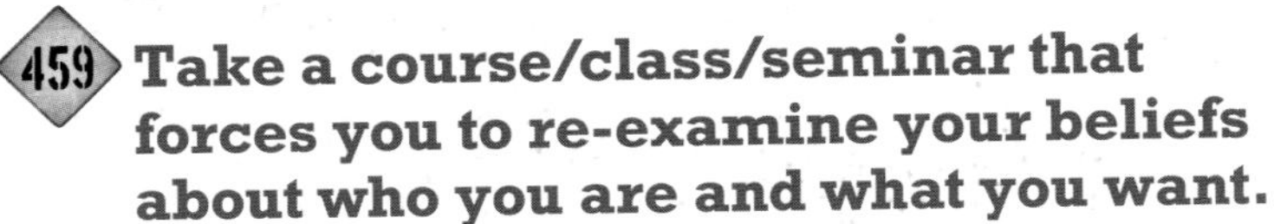

459 Take a course/class/seminar that forces you to re-examine your beliefs about who you are and what you want.

Every now and then, it's good to shake up your life by having a glance at the possible disparity between what you say you want, and what it is you really want. Go in with an open mind. If nothing else, it may reinvigorate your interest in what you're already doing.

460 Find an intelligent person diametrically opposed to one of your fundamental beliefs; carry on a rational, calm, logical conversation about that belief.

Defend your belief with sane argument. Nothing you believe is worth a damn unless you can coherently verbalize a cogent, objective thesis, supported by evidence and facts. No yelling.

461 Go get a college degree.

☠☠☠

College is about validating what it is you think and claim to know, and proving that you can demonstrate the patience and hardship of working toward a goal with delayed gratification. So put up with those lousy professors, do the reading, and turn in your homework. You'll be pleased with yourself for doing so.

462 Solve a mystery.

☠–☠☠☠☠☠, depending on conditions

No, it doesn't have to be a murder, or even a fantastic crime or anything. Sometimes you can just do research to come up with an answer someone else overlooked, and discover the reason something occurred.

START WITH A SMALL MYSTERY: MAYBE YOU CAN FIND MY MISSING CAR KEYS, FOR EXAMPLE.

463 Play a round of bingo with a host of people over the age of sixty.

☠☠

Don't play around and don't crack jokes. They can smell weakness, and will denigrate and exploit it. And for the sake of your own feeble life, no matter what, do not call a false bingo.

464 Sit through someone else's religious service.

☠ ☠ ☠

Try to politely observe a different rite than the one with which you're comfortable, without being completely judgmental and patronizing. Find one dramatically disparate from your own. Endure it. Go ahead and be judgmental.

465 Accept—and meet—a deadline.

☠ - ☠ ☠ ☠, depending on circumstances

Labeling, measuring, and cataloging time is an artifice invented by humans. But now that we've decided to recognize temporal distinctions, you are in the position to decide if you're going to play along. If you accept a deadline for any kind of project or endeavor, folks are going to expect you to follow through. So do it—you said you would.

Learn a foreign language.

You're probably pretty comfortable with your native tongue. It's something you understand, something you don't have to think about too much. Now try that all over again with another vocabulary and syntax.

WANT TO BE REALLY DARING? TRY A LANGUAGE WITH AN ENTIRELY DIFFERENT ALPHABET, LIKE RUSSIAN OR KOREAN.

Invent your own language.

It's been tried, and it's failed consistently. Language is messy, difficult, and full of exceptions to each inane rule. For some reason, a new, ordered, precise language has never supplanted any of the naturally occurring ones. Except among fourteen-year-old girls, who seem to have a genetic knack for this. Ben Franklin tried it, and it never caught on—what makes you think you can pull it off?

Learn a purely visual language.

Pick your favorite: American Sign Language, maritime signal flags, semaphore, etc., etc. Think of what a hit you'll be at parties.

469 Update to a new technology, even after you've spent your entire life with an archaic form, and are totally unprepared for the change.

This is an element of modern life, and will continue even more rapidly in the coming years. You're going to have to push yourself outside your comfort level, or risk being left behind financially and socially. Yes, it's time to lose the typewriter, Hoss. Ask a fourteen-year-old to help you.

470 Learn higher math.

It's a tricky set of rules, but once your brain is trained to think logically and objectively, it's not as hard as you might initially believe.

471 Learn advanced calculus.

"Imaginary numbers"? Enough said.

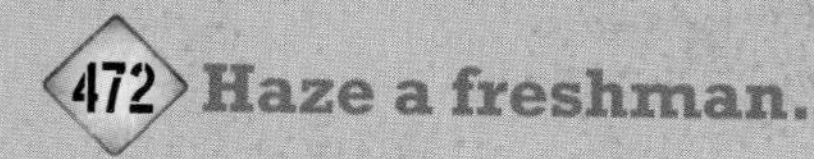

472 Haze a freshman.

☠☠☠

There's a time-honored tradition of making those new entrants into the realm of higher education perform some amazingly goofy and humiliating acts. Not that we should stand on tradition and call that sufficient reason; instead, look at the freshman itself: a pathetic, smarmy, beggared organism, created solely for the abuse. So call it performing nature's bidding.

473 Maintain use of an obsolete technology.

☠☠

The world has passed you by, and the utility of the thing is decreasing every day. But you're comfortable with it, and it works for you, so why bother changing to something newer?

THAT NEW THING IS GOING TO BE OBSOLETE IN EIGHTEEN MONTHS, AND YOU'RE GOING TO HAVE TO RELEARN HOW TO USE THE NEXT TECHNOLOGY, ANYWAY.

474 Stick to a personal conviction, even in the face of overwhelming public disapproval.

It's easy to be sure and right and true when you're surrounded by a mob of gainsayers involved in some serious groupthink. Now try it among the competition, adversaries, or enemy. Say what you mean, and don't back down.

475 Personally confront someone in power.

Teacher, politician, cop, employer, judge, parent—it doesn't matter. Stand up to them, challenge their authority, tell them when they're wrong. But make damned sure you're correct before you do it.

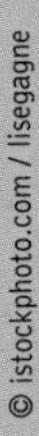

PLEASURE/PAIN THINGS Our bodies are linked to our minds in a countless number of ways and influence our perception of reality. The greatest motivators are our sense of pain and pleasure. Exploit them—make them work for you. See what they can really do.

476 Confront the thing you are most afraid of.

We've all got phobias—those things that make you cringe, even though you know there's no way the thing you're afraid of could harm you to the extent you fear it. Pick the biggest one.

GO AND DO SOMETHING, ANYTHING, THAT WILL PUSH YOU BEYOND YOUR TOLERATION LEVEL OF HEEBIE-JEEBIES.

477 Visit a brothel.

The single most honest sexual encounter you will ever have.

478 Set fire to something you once held dear.

Immolation is a time-honored means of converting a tangible thing to memory only. You can do this with just about anything (assuming it's not alive), and the practice has that poetic flair, with the bonus of catharsis.

479 Undergo an invasive surgical procedure involving full anesthesia.

☠☠

There is nothing quite like coming up out of the narcoticized blur. . . . It's not like waking up at all. Instead, you're suddenly just Somewhere Else than you were a moment ago, but now you've got a sore throat and some additional pain where they just cut you open.

480 Undergo an invasive surgical procedure involving no anesthesia.

☠☠☠☠

This is an egregiously evil custom, which some parents—and those persons allergic to, or otherwise hesitant about, anesthesia—elect for certain patients.

YOUR BRAIN IS NOT EQUIPPED TO DEAL WITH THIS FORM OF BARBARISM AND WILL RAIL AGAINST WHAT IS TAKING PLACE. AS WELL IT SHOULD.

481 Walk on hot coals.

☠

This is not daring at all; it's just a simple demonstration of certain physical principles, such as, "Gee, if I don't stand on the coals, they might not have enough time to burn me."

Try to re-enact Ben Franklin's famous experiment with lightning.

☠☠☠☠☠

It's quite apparent to most scholars that Franklin was grounded when he performed his feat, or he would have ended up a crispy critter. Several imitators who tried the stunt in the months following Franklin's performance wound up quite dead.

Stay awake for forty-eight hours straight, in the wilderness.

☠☠☠

The variety and intensity of sounds that occur naturally in the wilderness are astounding—and are bound to wig you out after you've gone a sufficient amount of time without sleep.

Endure a sweat lodge.

☠☠–☠☠☠☠, depending on conditions

This is usually a hut made of natural materials in which heated rocks are placed, and continually refreshed, to keep the temperature high and the atmosphere stifling. The longer you can remain inside, the more daring.

INGESTION THINGS Your mouth, esophagus, and stomach are the gateways to your digestive system, and, from there, to your entire body. Remember the old aphorism from the computer-processing field: GIGO ("Garbage In, Garbage Out"). Makes sense, doesn't it?

485 Eat an ice cream cone as fast as you can.

☠

You're crazy—you're out of control. Stop now, before you hurt someone—including yourself.

486 Eat something from a street vendor.

☠

Botulism. Salmonella. Dyspepsia. These are words created and disseminated by the evil adversaries of fun and good times. They know nothing of what is Right and Wonderful. A hot dog from a Chicago corner cart, in season, far and away exceeds the deliciousness of steak tartare at a fancy restaurant. Some say a hot dog with a sporting event in front of it is the prime delicacy; they are also wrong.

487 Eat an insect. Or a bug—like a worm.

☠ ☠ ☠

Squeeze out the gooey dirt-by-product first. Try the big red ants; they have a lemony aftertaste. And, yes, covering them in chocolate is cheating.

Enter an eating contest.

☠ ☠ ☠

There are all kinds, from your standard county fair pie-eating competition, to the professional how-many-sticks-of-butter-can-you-put-away-in-three-minutes. Ergh. There's actually a circuit for this kind of thing, as the prizes are surprisingly valuable.

IT SEEMS THAT BODY MASS HAS NOTHING TO DO WITH CONSUMPTION CAPACITY, AS SOME OF THE BEST PERFORMERS ARE SKINNY FOLK.

Drink enough alcohol to get you drunk.

☠

Again, not all that complicated, one would think. The catch, of course, is that as you're drinking, and getting closer to drunk, your desire—and wherewithal—for remembering to stop drinking is impaired.

Try a keg stand.

☠

File under "Stupid College Tricks." Have some friends hold you, inverted, over a keg of beer. Place your mouth on the nozzle. Quaff as much as you possibly can. No, I don't understand it either.

491 Do a beer bong.

☠

Also known colloquially as the "shotgun" technique, this involves gravity, pressure, and the mystic forces of idiocy that infest young people, particularly when it comes to ingesting large amounts of mood-altering consumables.

492 Ingest a substance currently prohibited by law in your own jurisdiction.

☠ ☠

Rumor has it that the thrills offered by these things, and the feelings they give, are well worth sacrificing such things as safety, quality control, and self-respect.

THESE DAYS, THE MOST INTERESTING DRUGS ARE MAINLY AVAILABLE FROM YOUR DOCTOR.

493 Become addicted to something; try to give it up cold turkey.

☠ ☠ ☠

Pick your poison: sugar, caffeine, nicotine. Get good and comfortable with it—let it become not just a joy, not just a habit, but a true need. Put it away for a week. Or a month. Hold out on yourself just for giggles. Resume in that welcoming, self-immolating junkie manner.

494 Make a soufflé.

☠☠

You got all the ingredients, mixed them properly, in the right order. You've got the oven set at the right temperature, for the proper duration. But that sucker still fell, didn't it?

495 Steal honey from wild bees.

☠☠☠

The bees don't care for this practice. And they will make you aware of it in the way that bees have of showing their displeasure. Repeatedly.

496 Drink the national drink in as many countries as possible.

☠☠☠

Soju in Korea. Aguardiente in Colombia. Sake in Japan. Vodka in Russia. It would seem that the national drinks of most countries are oily, violent, clear liquids, intended to either inebriate the drinker or cauterize wounds.

#496

497 Raise honeybees.

☠ ☠ ☠

For the honey, of course. Not, I mean, so that you have an entire colony of vicious little creatures who will do your bidding at your whim. Because they won't—bees aren't docile enough to become evil hench-creatures. Darn.

498 Go spicy.

☠ – ☠ ☠ ☠, depending on conditions

Many sources claim to have "the world's spiciest [whatever]." I'm always wary of anyone who makes a statement involving exclusivity and/or extremity without qualifiers. Still, if you and your intestinal tract are up to it, try to out-spice your palate without causing any second-degree burns. Make it as powerful as you can stand.

WASABI, HABANERO AND OTHER CHILI PEPPERS, HORSE-RADISH, CURRY, GARLIC, GINGER, AND MUSTARD CAN BE COMBINED INTO A DISH THAT CAN TRULY HARM YOU.

499 Drink Turkish coffee.

☠☠☠

Might as well mainline the concoction by shooting it straight into an artery. This is a no foolin', high-octane kick in the kidneys, and it will jazz you on several levels, both with the muddy caffeine and the treacly sweetener. Don't play with this.

500 Drink Irish coffee.

☠☠☠

Because uppers alone are not enough to entice you, add a downer to the mix; in this case, alcohol combined with caffeine and sugar. Howdy.

501 Drink some tea.

☠

The choice of sophisticated palates, among caffeinated beverages. Really, the worst risk here is that you'll be accused of being British.

ABOUT THE AUTHOR

On a $20 bet, the author jumped out a second-story high school window when he was seventeen. He tore some cartilage in his left knee. Unfortunately, he did not learn from the financial disparity of this experience and has since done a bunch of silly things. He's flown a glider and a Cessna; rappelled down a cliff face and out of a hovering helicopter; driven a race car; dumped a motorcycle; nearly drowned while trying to learn to surf (ditto water-skiing); went scuba-diving off the Great Barrier Reef; slalomed double black diamond runs in the Rocky Mountains; rafted class IV rapids and canoed Class III; gone the distance in numerous boxing matches and other martial arts events (and lost just as many times); run with a herd of bulls at the request of his crazed editor; fired the combined small-arms inventory of both NATO and the former Warsaw Pact; visited brothels on five continents; eaten a variety of bizarre things (including rattlesnake, horseflesh, and something that was still moving); supplied security services to the FBI, Department of Defense, and Department of Homeland Security; worked as an undercover investigative journalist; served as a military officer on classified counterdrug operations; and maintained a long-term relationship with a redhead.

He admits he might be stupid.